LOVING

The Mystical Heart of Success

LOVING: The Mystical Heart of Success
Published 2020 by Your Book Angel
Copyright ©

All rights reserved. No part of this book may be reproduced, stored, or transmitted by any means—whether auditory, graphic, mechanical, or electronic—without written permission of both publisher and author, except in the case of brief excerpts used in critical articles and reviews. Unauthorized reproduction of any part of this work is illegal and is punishable by law.

Printed in the United States
Edited by Keidi Keating
Layout by Rochelle Mensidor

ISBN: 978-1-7341814-6-3

INTRODUCTION

I remember being a little girl aged around six or seven. The grown-ups in my life would ask me, "What do you want to be when you grow up?" As a little girl (and later, as a big girl), I had a very vivid, fertile imagination. I would answer that I was going to be rich and famous, marry a great man, have bunches of happy kids, write books, teach people, heal people, and so on.

Upon completion of my thorough and enthusiastic account of "what I want to be when I grow up," all of these grown-ups would laugh uproariously and say, "Get real, Virginia!" My mother, if she happened to be present, would say, "What makes you think you're any better than the rest of us? You'll end up poor and miserable like we are, and you'll like it!"

I'd swallow hard and try not to cry at this pronouncement of my impending "doom and gloom," and somewhere inside of me I'd promise myself that wasn't true. But part of me believed what these grown-ups told me. In frustration and fear, and *in trust*, I slowly buried my "irrational," "impractical," "better than other people" dreams and created my life from the same fabric of misery and poverty that cloaked my family. I was miserable and unhappy, but at least I fit in; at least I was loved and accepted by the grown-ups in my life, or so I thought.

As I grew up, I noticed that, in fact, I could never seem to please those dark, unhappy beings I curried favor from. I could never be miserable enough, poor enough, sick enough, or anything else "enough." I discovered that, in addition to being angry, dissatisfied, and unhappy like the rest of them, I was also expected to be creative, wise, and generous, making the grown-ups feel better by listening to their problems and coming up with effective, insightful solutions. What a dilemma! How was I to do both—be sad, miserable, and unsuccessful like the rest of them, but also lead them down a better path? This conundrum was a source of inestimable frustration for many years.

One day I realized I had misunderstood. I had misinterpreted the grown-ups' speeches of foreboding and "doom and gloom." They had never meant their statements to be a set of instructions on how I should live my life. They were simply sharing their pain and confusion. They were telling me they did not know how to help themselves, and so they could not help me. They were pushing me to see the Light and help myself. They were challenging me to find a way to make my dreams come true, if I could and if I dared.

They were warning me that such a path would be difficult, if I chose to take it. If I was to find and follow the dreams of my heart, I would need to trust myself 100 per cent, possibly with no external approval. I would need to make choices that seemed contrary to everything I had ever witnessed or been taught. I would need to unquestionably stand with and for myself, loving myself, and supporting myself as I went along. But, if I chose to do that, I could, against all odds, live my sweetest dreams. And then again, if I chose to, I could help them—the grown-ups—and later my children, by setting an example of what can be done if one loves and believes in oneself enough to try. If I chose to, and if I dared.

Well, I did dare, and I do every day. Every day, from a place of being very human, and at times, weighed down, discouraged, and overwhelmed by the world and the negative teachings I have received all my life, I reach into my Heart, rediscover my dreams, and create a life I love, enjoy, and am proud of...and you can too! I'd like to assist you with that process in this book.

SECTION ONE

SUCCESS AND THE HEART

CHAPTER ONE
SUCCESS

"Success is everyone's heritage." ~John-Roger

The idea that no one is born to fail is very appealing, but what does that actually mean? Does it mean we were all born with silver spoons in our mouths? (We know that's not so!) Does it mean that we will *all* be rich and famous someday? (Is that realistic or desirable?) Does it mean that none of us will ever fall flat on our faces or not manifest what we think we want regardless of how hard we try? I don't think so. And, just looking around me, I would say that the evidence in the world and most people's lives concurs with my opinion. But, that said, I also think that John-Roger's statement was presenting a truth—perhaps even the Truth (with a capital "T")—that success is deeply and innately present in and for every human being.

Most of us would find it difficult to believe wholeheartedly in this perception of reality, either because we perceive that we've failed at one time or another, and/or because we expect to fail at some point in the future. We believe, somewhere inside of us, that failure is an intrinsic part of life, and somehow, easier to accomplish than success. We theorize that successful people are either born lucky or work very, very hard for what they get. We suspect that they often sacrifice other "more important things," such as their health, family relationships, moral criterion, and so on, in order to create any material success they achieve in their lives—material success that most of us, at some level, want for ourselves. Either way, it seems that wealth and success are either a matter of grace (and, thus, outside of our control)—or very expensive in terms of the human soul.

But is that true? Is *real* success either bequeathed by the gods or paid for with the sacrifice of more meaningful aspects of our lives? I think not—and I say that as a person who has been exposed to diverse aspects of the success-poverty continuum.

I was born into a family of very mixed fortunes. My maternal grandfather began his life as the son of a poor dirt-farmer in Missouri. He never finished fourth grade, yet he went on to become a self-made multi-millionaire. He was a well-known business icon in the Pennsylvania County I grew up in. He owned hotels, shopping malls, apartment buildings, multiple companies, working farms, and even an operational West Virginia plantation.

However, his children and grandkids called his money "poison" and "blood-money." From his family's perspective, my grandfather had "sold his soul" to make money. Rumor had it that his first wife, my mom's mom, had died under "mysterious circumstances," allowing my grandfather to marry a woman who brought increased financial wealth to their partnership. This second wife had no desire to raise my mom and her sister, and mistreated them, leaving both girls hurt and angry with her and their father. With his new wife's help, my grandfather managed to alienate both of his daughters.

He also allowed one set of his grandchildren to be put in an orphanage rather than assist his eldest daughter, my mother, in a time of need. Years later, he would pull strings with his cronies at the bank to force that daughter into foreclosure and ultimately bankruptcy, because he wanted to add some property she owned (the first home she ever had that she loved) to his portfolio.

My grandfather did similar hurtful and destructive things to his other daughter and her family, as well as to an indeterminate number of other people, both strangers and business associates. He simply did not think twice about hurting or even destroying people if it would net him a profit or satisfy a grudge. Many people referred to my grandfather as "heartless." I found it rather symbolic that he had suffered eight heart attacks by the time he was fifty, and several more before one killed him in his early seventies.

Even in death my grandfather continued to lash out at those he claimed to care about. All his life, he proclaimed loudly that his altruistic motive for building his empire was to take care of and leave it all to his family. However, in his will he left all his money to his last mistress, and nothing to his kids or grandchildren. When he died none of his family attended his funeral, nor cared to attend the reading of his will.

My grandfather had a lot of money. He pretty much owned all the "stuff" he wanted to own. To this day, he has streets, apartment buildings, and shopping malls named after him. He had undisputed power in a certain arena. He could manifest anything he wanted and everyone in the mid-sized town and county he lived in knew that and respected that ability. But, was he rich? Was he honestly wealthy? Was he successful? The answer to those questions depends on how one defines riches, wealth, and success, doesn't it?

A related story from the other end of the spectrum: My mother, as I have shared, was born into a family that would ultimately become very wealthy, materially. But in the midst of that, she was verbally, emotionally, and physically mistreated. She had a complete psychological breakdown when she was eighteen years old. After shock treatments, therapy, and medication, she was released. She desperately sought someone to love her and make her life better. She met, fell in love with, and married a handsome, charming man, who unfortunately turned out to be more interested in her family's fortune than in being kind to her. He continued the abuse she had grown up with, adding infidelity to the mix. When my mom was pregnant with their second child, my grandfather informed her husband that there was no way he'd ever get his hands on any of the family money. So my dad left my mom and never went back. He also connived his way out of paying child support.

My mom worked hard as a hotel maid and waitress, until the strain and pressure of trying to survive pushed her into another breakdown when she was in her mid-twenties. Because my grandfather had so much net worth, my mom was not eligible for the usual state aid for mothers and children in our position. My grandfather did little to help her. My sister and I were eventually put in a church-run orphanage, while our mother was hospitalized.

Five years later, my mom had pretty much recovered and remarried. My sister and I went back to live with her. Her new husband was a hard-working, uneducated laborer. They strove to build a new life together. They disdained people who built their lives around power and money; people like my grandfather. This attitude could have been a good thing. It could have led them to build a life around loving and values of the heart.

However, unfortunately, my mom and stepdad rejected money and wealth from a place of hurt, anger, and bitterness. They felt victimized and poor. Those feelings colored their entire lives, so that no matter what they did or what they had, they stayed poor in every way—and deeply unhappy. Their values were values of being *against* wealth and success. This position caused them to spiral into a deep pit of rage, despair, and helplessness. They hated anyone who was remotely successful, which of course alienated them from people like that, and from the potential inside themselves to be like those people. I think sometimes they forgot what happiness, and even the love between them, was all about.

This story is clearly not one of material wealth. More importantly, to me, it is also not a story of *inner wealth*. Instead, it is a story about the myth of rejecting material success as a pathway to inner riches. It exemplifies what happens if one takes this approach from bitterness, hurt, anger, and feelings of lack. Rejecting material wealth and worldly success can become a poisonous state that eventually destroys love and any sense of goodness and value in one's life. It can prove to be no more noble, healthy, joy-producing or effective than the greed and selfishness that drove my grandfather.

Now, another perspective. This is not a perfect example, but perhaps another way to look at success and wealth. I was born into the family I have described—a family with extreme variances of wealth and poverty. I was put in an orphanage when I was five and stayed there until I was ten, when my mom remarried. My stepdad was basically a good person, as was my mom. I believe he and my mom loved each other, but, as I said, they often focused on only their shared disdain of money and wealth. In some ways they took pride in being poor, working folks who always struggled to survive. Money was extremely tight all the time. As a result, there were also many fights about money and a lot of fear expressed about whether or not they could make ends meet. There was no sense of fun and creativity in the home—just fear and concerns about our survival, and anger that sometimes escalated into intense physical and verbal violence. That became the theme of their, and our, existence. Not the love that had originally brought them together.

There was also always a lot of drama in our household and our extended family about my grandfather's wealth and power, and how that impacted everyone. As I mentioned previously, my grandfather seemed to love using his assets to cripple his family members' ability to create their own success. Perhaps that was because he wanted the control, power, and reverence he thought being a rich patriarch would gain for him. I don't know. I never really understood the way he thought and behaved.

What I do know is that his children and grandchildren pulled away from him, refusing gifts, refusing money, refusing jobs, and (for me) refusing to let him pay for a college education, because all of us were very clear that accepting anything from him had unpleasant strings attached. Accepting his gifts always gave him the power to rescind the gifts and to hurt and betray us any way he could, if the mood so struck him—or if he stood to profit or gain power from it. The hurt, anger, and bitterness that resulted from how my grandfather interacted with his family colored all of our lives in very profound ways. It was expressed in our homes as physical and verbal abuse, and it reflected into the world as a rejection of material success, and subsequently, as the manifestation of poverty and failure.

I left home when I was eighteen years old. I definitely had mixed feelings about money and "worldly success," but I was clear that I wanted happiness, kindness, love, peace, fun, and beauty in my life. I didn't much care about money. I simply had not seen it do anyone much good.

My twenties were spent around artists, musicians, and people of various alternative spiritual paths. I wrote; I painted; I danced; I married multiple times; and had kids far too young, but I also had fun, meaningfulness, love, thoughtfulness, and creativity in my life. The fact that money came and went—sometimes too quickly— hardly mattered to me because lots of other good stuff was present. My world seemed light when compared with my childhood, and I was pretty happy.

As I grew older, I remarried (again), held more traditional jobs, and embarked on various entrepreneurial endeavors. Money came and money went. Sometimes I had lots of money and sometimes very little—but my life was always an adventure and fun! It was based on personal growth and development, on knowing Spirit personally, on cultivating Loving as a way of being and a way of life, on doing service, and on building a family and friendship group that was kind and full of intimacy, honesty, trust, laughter, learning, and fun. *Those* were the things I wanted, so those were the things I *chose* to build my life around.

So far, sixty years in, my life has been good. I think that is because what mattered to me most was love, kindness, trust, service, growing, learning, peace, adventure, spirit, and fun—and simply being a good person doing good wherever I could. Because I chose that and focused on it, my life was full of those qualities and experiences that matched them. *That* became my experience of wealth—and whether money was present or not didn't matter so much. I always had enough for myself, and enough to share. As my four lovely daughters put it now that they are grown, sometimes the circumstances of our lives together were challenging, but we always had each other. And we always had *fun*. My kids always knew they were loved, by me and by those we allowed into our life. Best of all—as they tell me often, I am and have always been a person they love and respect. That, for me, especially when compared to my childhood, and my mother and granddad's lives and relationships with their kids, constitutes great success!

I want to be clear that I did a lot of inner work to create this life for myself, and to become the person I am and wanted to be. I chose a non-conventional spiritual path by the time I was twenty-one, and I have always maintained that path. Its practices and meditations are a plumb-line for me in my life. I did lots of personal growth workshops and many different kinds of therapy. I applied everything helpful and healing I could find in books and life to re-create myself into a person who could have the kind of life I wanted to live. It wasn't always easy or pain-free, but I was determined that the course and tone of my life (and my kids') was not going to be determined by what I had witnessed growing up, nor by the beliefs and guidelines I had learned through that witnessing.

So, all that said, the question I am posing to you at this point; the question that for me was a starting point of creating a life I loved and was happy with, is this: What is success, really? It is easy to say that everyone deserves success, and that no one was put on Earth to "fail"—but what does that mean? *What is success?*

From my experience, different people define success differently. Because of that variance, different people also define failure differently. Since the perception of failure is often simply a by-product of how one defines success, and because "success" is the positive focus we want to develop and the goal we aspire to, let's begin by exploring the meaning of success.

Some people define success as mega-money, expensive cars, big houses, real estate, power, fame, awards, prestige or the "right" mate. For others it is simpler: marriage, family, job, vacations, a savings account, or sending their kids through college. Still others have different, even seemingly negative definitions, such as "conquering" others financially, emotionally or sexually, having another drink or cigarette, or getting around the laws of the land without getting into trouble. Some people even define success as my mom and stepdad did: being poor and using that to say "up yours" to wealthy people who may have hurt or betrayed them. (My parents were very "successful" at not being like my grandfather, and later, at not giving him any more power or opportunities to hurt them.) All of these are variations of the same theme. All of them are definitions (though the latter are somewhat distorted) of "external success."

To some people, these aspects of success are far more important than any others, and I want to be clear that there is nothing wrong with wanting outer symbols of success. I myself, however, might qualify that statement, because of my experiences, by adding "as long as it doesn't hurt anyone." And, I will also say that getting what one wants and then seeing or feeling that it caused yourself or others pain, can be a positive, transformative step forward, if one chooses to be honest about what happened and then use that awareness to become a better person and to create more helpful experiences. But, for the purpose of this book, I want to suggest that it may be more effective right from the beginning to approach manifesting outer success in conjunction with focusing upon manifesting inner success also.

Inner success is often described using words such as integrity, satisfaction, love, kindness, truth, peace, generosity, contentment, courage, and so on. People who define success primarily in these terms would generally agree with Carolyn Hillman when she says, "Success is being happy first with yourself, and then with your life." Some people believe these inner dimensions of success are not only more important than the outer, but, really, they are *the only* true measures of success.

Most of us, in all honesty, would define success as somewhat of a blend of both of these points of view. I would say, if we look closely, we would discover that when we look to the outer world to define what we want (for example, "I want a lot of money"), we are looking for a form through which to express or manifest an inner quality (for example, self-worth, freedom or security). In this world, on planet Earth, the inner state and the outer form are inextricably intertwined. Reaching for one inevitably puts us in contact with the other. Perhaps the key to real success is recognizing which is most important and which needs to come first for us in our asking, doing, and receiving.

In my opinion, success is possibly not the easiest, but certainly one of the most natural experiences we can give ourselves, as natural as breathing our next breath and allowing ourselves to be the very best of who we really are. We simply do not believe this is true and/or we don't know how to do it. So we need to be reminded. We need to re-learn what success really is.

CHAPTER TWO
THE HEART

> "All paths are the same; they lead nowhere. Ask yourself and yourself alone...'Does this path have a heart?' If it does, the path is good. If it doesn't, it is of no use. One makes for a joyful journey...the other will make you curse your life." ~ Carlos Castaneda

There is a spiritual center inside of each of us. In that center our entire spiritual heritage is stored, our connectedness with the Source of all Life, and the remembrance of who we really are—Children of God, Children of Love. Leo Buscaglia notes, "Love and the self are one, and the discovery of either is the realization of both." The Bhagavad Gita reiterates, "Within the Heart resides the True Dweller within the body." The discovery of this "True Dweller" and the realization of our loving selves are one and the same thing. Both exist as a Presence within the Heart. Becoming aware of who we really are and of our place in the universe is empowering. That awareness allows us to access and utilize an endless source of energy, as we will discover.

The Heart also serves to connect us with the world and other living beings. It is the source of our most authentic relationship with the planet and its inhabitants. We gain certain sensitivities through the Heart that allow us to more effectively interact with others, both for their advancement and ours. These sensitivities and awarenesses also contribute to an ecological and compassionate utilization of the energy we can access through our "True Dweller."

Our Hearts hold the knowledge of our purposes on Earth, as well as an intuitive overview of the purpose of the planet. Information and guidance about what we need to do here to fulfill our highest destinies and to manifest the planetary potential are available to us through an intimate, yet practical connection with this spiritual center. Because of this function of the Heart, it operates as the source of our wisdom, our vision and, ultimately, our success.

Ancient metaphysical "mystery schools" taught that the human body and consciousness exist first, and ultimately, as energy. (Metaphysics is the branch of philosophy that investigates the nature of core principles and problems of ultimate reality, including the study of the Beingness and structure of the universe.) This energy vibrates at a variety of frequencies. Each frequency correlates to a different aspect of human existence. For example, the energy that shapes the physical body vibrates at a different speed and on a different wavelength than the energy that shapes the mind or emotions. The particles of energy, and the aspects of consciousness they shape and represent, relate to levels of the "aura" (the electromagnetic field that surrounds and interpenetrates the human body). Each level of the aura anchors into the physical body at a particular site related to an endocrine gland. These anchor points are called "chakras" or energy centers.

The Heart is considered to be the fourth energy center or chakra. It is anchored into the physical form at the thymus. It is said to express "paraconsciousness," that is, the aspect of human consciousness beyond consciousness. It is believed that through the heart center we are able to access that which is beyond our everyday scope of reality and awareness.

The paraconsciousness that is available to us through the heart center is multi-aspected. One aspect of it is "intuition," and another may be termed "Divine Guidance." Bertrand Babinet teaches that it is through the Heart we are able to access Spirit directly, and then mobilize the Love that is innately its essence. This Love, in its flow or movement from formless to formed, becomes Lov-ing. When we are in alignment with this Loving, and the awareness that goes with it, we are more easily able to utilize it as a guiding force in our lives.

There are also other "extra-sensory" abilities available to us as a result of connecting to the Heart, abilities such as clairaudience, clairvoyance, and clairsentience (the power to hear, see, and feel that which is outside of the natural range of human senses). When we access these abilities though the Heart (rather than through the psychic centers), we are guided in their usage by the innate kindness and wisdom of Spirit. These gifts become *spiritual* gifts (rather than psychic) that exist in relationship to a consciousness of Loving, which precludes them being misused or harmful. These extended abilities can result in an expanded experience of Spirit, God, and the Universe. Many of the recorded mystical, spiritual experiences of saints and other chosen individuals have been a result of these individuals accessing the spiritual energy through a focus of devotion, loving, and purity of Heart.

A related experience available through the Heart is that of "empathy," a deep identification with and understanding of another person's situations, feelings, and motives. I want to differentiate this quality from that of "sympathy," which is an affinity between people or things, in which *whatever affects one affects the other.* Sympathy is not a desirable state. It does not allow us to honestly assess, assist, and support others; but generally involves jumping in the other person's pit with them.

Empathy, on the other hand, allows us to see clearly and with compassion the plight of other human beings, but without being *adversely affected* by it—that is, *without going through it with them,* emotionally, psychically or physically. Empathy offers us a perspective from which we can more effectively interact with other people. Empathy can help us to see the "rope" that might assist our comrades in escaping from their pits of negativity, misunderstanding or misperception, and gives us the caring to throw it to them. This form of loving and caring is a quality of the Heart. Many spiritual teachers call it compassion or loving "for the highest good of all concerned."

To me, loving "for the highest good" is very similar to the love of an honestly caring, effective parent. The parent offers their child not only what he/she wants, but also what he/she *needs* to be whole, healthy and happy, and then, to mix metaphors, the parent teaches the child to fish for his/her own wholeness, health, wealth, and happiness, instead of feeding it to him/her forever. Empathy allows us to make that quality available in all of our relationships, with the man on the street, lovers, significant others, parents, coworkers, friends, and ourselves. Expressing this quality of loving can enhance our relationships with both others and ourselves. Loving in this way can assist us in creating relational success that is truly satisfying.

The Heart, from my perspective acts as a pivotal point for the spiritual and personal aspects of humankind. The Heart transmutes the earth energies and experiences into spiritual energies and experiences, and vice versa. When we examine what goes on for us in our day-to-day lives, and gain spiritual awareness—that is, an awareness of the Loving that is present in all of life (I also call this wisdom)—we learn from our experiences. When we do not take our experiences "to heart" and learn from them, we tend to repeat our lessons over and over again. When we take the guidance, loving and awareness of our Hearts back into our life experiences, we enhance those experiences. Our lives and relationships tend to work better, partially because our attitudes and approaches are more conducive to bringing forward positive results. When we do not activate spiritual awareness in our lives, even if we get what we want in the world, usually the qualities of peace, joy, and satisfaction are missing. We thus lose the opportunity to experience success from the inside out...and from the outside in again.

There is value in both the spiritual and personal aspects of life; indeed, both of these are integral pieces of what we are here on Earth for. If we are loving God/Spirit and allowing God/Spirit to love us, and then loving ourselves and, additionally, sharing that loving with the world and receiving back what the world has to offer, we are fulfilling our purposes here. We are also living a powerful formula for success.

Exactly how we accomplish this balanced flow of loving is unique for each individual. The specific nature of all of these relationships is determined initially by our relationships with the Loving and with our Hearts. The quality and quantity of our loving *for* Spirit determines the quality and quantity of Loving that we are capable of receiving back *from* Spirit. If we love only a little, or give that loving as a test with many conditions, the loving we receive in return seems to reflect that, because that's all that we can perceive.

Imagine being an eyedropper, giving a drop of loving to Spirit. Even if Spirit responded by sending us an ocean of Loving (and It does!), we would be capable of receiving only an eyedropper-full, because that eyedropper is all we believe ourselves to be. To paraphrase Meister Eckhart: The Heart through which I love God is the same Heart through which God loves me.

If that eyedropper-full of Loving is all that we are capable of receiving, then that is also all that we have available to fill ourselves with. There, resultantly, is little or no overflow, little or nothing for us to share with the world. Because of natural law, namely, "For every action, there is an equal and opposite reaction," that eyedropper-full then becomes all the world can give back to us. By our own hands, because of a complex system of beliefs, emotional patterns, and negative imaging, we become paupers, instead of kings and queens. As we have sown, so do we reap.

This process begins and ends in the Heart, and the good news is, we can do it differently. We can passionately open our Hearts to embrace the Loving, first by simply *whole-heartedly choosing* to do that. This naturally places God/Spirit/the Divine/the One or Love, where it belongs—FIRST ("Thou shalt have no other God before me." Exodus 20:2). By then receiving into ourselves the Presence that comes forward through this process and by taking that Presence and Its qualities deeply into ourselves, we place ourselves where we need to be, in the Spirit of Loving, next to God, and in a position to be our own best friends. As the Presence fills us, the abundance of Loving, and the health, wealth, and happiness that go with it, will naturally extend into the world as overflow.

In other words, ultimately, filtered through our unique individuality, this Loving becomes our expression and our work in the world. Because we filled ourselves with God, we now have much to give, and we give that naturally and automatically. Then, through the same natural law that limited our results previously, we now also have much to receive. Even more importantly, because our Hearts are already filled with the Loving and the abundance of Spirit, that which we reap in the world becomes "icing on the cake." We have the Fullness within us—the True Dweller—as soon as we are consciously connected with the Heart, Spirit, and the Loving.

What does all this have to do with success? *That Fullness is our Inner Success.* The results we reap when that extends into the world become our outer success. Everything is energy, including Loving. Spirit has *only* unmanifested Energy to offer us. That goes forward into the world (shaped by our practical reasoning and effective actions) and comes back to us as the only thing the world has to give—manifested energy or *form* (our houses, cars, loved ones, money, and so on). Our jobs are simply to connect with the Source of the Energy/the Loving to become deep, full reservoirs for that, and then to use our feelings, thoughts, bodies, and imaginations to direct it in the most effective way, always receiving from Spirit and giving to the world. Our Hearts are the tools and vehicles for that connection and the reservoirs for the Loving. They also help guide us on how to best utilize our feelings, thoughts, bodies, and imaginations in our activities in the world.

So, how do we do all this, exactly? Tara Singh suggests, "Put your idealism away; get to know yourself." We can only discover our Hearts, and our individual and unique "paths of Heart" if we are willing to look deeply inside and acknowledge those parts of ourselves that are not in alignment with that. If we do this, *with love*, those parts will naturally be healed and reprogrammed. We can then utilize them to re-access the Source of the Loving, and to create our success. But, to begin, we need to discover the places within us and our lives where the Loving is not, and take it there.

We also need to know and acknowledge where the Loving *is* with celebration. We need, with joy, to remind ourselves of our successes, those riches of Heaven and Earth that are already present for us. We need to discover and bring to the forefront those healed places in us where the Loving and our Hearts are already expressing and manifesting fully, so that we can use them as reference points for our future growth.

As part of these processes, we need to access and utilize the Loving Heart that is present within us so that it can serve as a guide to the healing that needs to be done, and to the techniques that can most effectively facilitate that. We need to allow our Hearts to discern for us our own unique visions of success and the particular expression of inner and outer health, wealth and happiness that exists for us, and then, to direct us to our personal path of fulfilling it. We need to go to our Hearts for all of that, rather than the world or other people's opinions. As Saint-Exupéry notes in *The Little Prince*, "It is only with the heart that one can see rightly; what is essential is invisible to the eye."

Each of us already has a success form inside of us. We may not be in touch with it, but it is there. We may not be able to see it with our physical eyes, but it can be seen through the Heart. That's faith: "evidence of that which is unseen." Bringing that unseen success into manifested form is simply a matter of loving ourselves enough to clear a channel through which it can come forward into reality for us to have, enjoy, and share.

In addition to learning to access our Hearts and keep the Loving present in our lives and consciousness, it is important to explore the shape, form, and substance of our personalized expressions of success in the world. We must know what we are and have been doing right. We need to recognize and acknowledge our current successes. Then we need to delineate the areas of our lives that need work, areas into which we would like to direct the Loving, and our Hearts' awareness, for healing, enhancement, and greater success.

Remember that our Hearts are our connecting points with Spirit and the channels through which the Loving flows through us and into the world. Our Hearts are also the sources of our intuitive knowing of what we need to do to fulfill our highest destinies, and to create our greatest successes.

Most of us have had experiences of Loving and being in our Hearts. We can use these experiences to create something that in Neuro-Linguistic Programming is called a "resource state." By simply remembering previous experiences of our Hearts and the Loving, and then touching a place on our bodies, we can create a physical anchor point which we can use to access our Hearts and the Loving whenever we need them.

Before we do this, I want to note that there are different aspects and qualities of Loving. In creating our resource states and anchor points, we want to make sure we are using experiences that are connected with the Heart. For most of us, when we feel "touched" by a person or experience, we naturally refer to the center of our chests to express where this deep connection is taking place. This is the point we want to access for our resource state; this is where our human experience of Loving lies.

We also have other experiences we refer to as love, which are centered in different parts of the body. Feelings associated with bonding and romantic love are, for the most part, energetically connected with the solar plexus, an area situated in the upper belly. Power, often associated with sexual love, is connected with a place in the lower belly, three finger widths below the naval. Dependency is generally connected with the umbilicus or belly button. In order to effectively access the healing, transformational, and co-creative power of Love we discussed earlier in this section, it is critical that we distinguish between these other aspects and those states of Loving clearly connected to the heart center in the middle of the chest.

CHAPTER THREE
CHALLENGES

> "Success means having the courage, the determination, and the will to become the person you believe you were meant to be." ~Sheehan

Let's take a moment to look at the obstacles we might initially face as we set off on this path of creating success through the Heart. The first challenge of creating success for ourselves is simply to be willing to create success for ourselves. Ha—a conundrum! Creating success for ourselves is, indeed, not as easy as it sounds. Most of us have been taught, to some degree, that it is unacceptable for us to have and enjoy more success than other people, particularly than the grown-ups who raised us. This is a difficult obstacle to overcome—misplaced loyalty. I struggled with it for years.

The second challenge of creating success is to define what that means *to us*, as opposed to what that means to other people. Our concepts of success have, for the most part, been shaped for us by the many authority figures in our lives. Their definitions and delusions were enshrined upon our Inner Altars before we were even old enough to realize how important this pastime of creating success was going to be to us. We need to un-enshrine those concepts, definitions, and delusions. We need to redefine success for ourselves. Regardless of what we were taught, from my experience, we always get what we ask for, and what we feel and think is important to us. And what we ask for and get reflects and defines us.

So—as your momma may have told you—be careful what you ask for. Or perhaps more accurately, *understand* what you are asking for and why you are asking for it—and perhaps tweak your request a bit. Then, once you have manifested your desire, look at it, learn what you can learn from it, and love it a lot!

Why? Because creating success and manifesting things and experiences here on Earth is just an awareness exercise—a personal growth exercise, if you will—a way to learn, express and become more of who we *really* are. And, in my opinion, by far the most powerful, fun, and effective way to approach this process is by walking the path hand-in-hand with Spirit. We need to claim the partnership between ourselves, in our many human and higher aspects, and the energy, essence and consciousness of the Universe that is within and all around us. This a partnership that has been recognized and taught for centuries by numerous esoteric schools focused on psycho-religious thought. The teachings of these "mystery schools" clarify the innate relationship between the structure of human consciousness, our awareness of the availability of Spirit in our lives, *and material success*. There are many modern alternative psychological and spiritual systems that agree with these ancient teachings; *The Law of Attraction* books have been one of the recent, popular versions of that.

My book will in some ways reiterate those teachings, as they are valuable and accurate—but this book is also different. Many of my clients and friends—and indeed I, myself—have expressed feeling somewhat frustrated by the deceptive simplicity of the New Age Success Teachings. First of all, there are *huge* differences in the processes of individuals who were born into and live in this world with very few challenges to face, and the processes of individuals who came into or developed situations and circumstances that can only be called difficult. I, as one of the latter individuals, found it hard to even contemplate writing this book, which is about creating a successful life by being and doing the *loving* that I believe and have experienced us all to be capable of and, indeed, are ultimately *destined* to be and do.

When I read *The Law of Attraction* books, I worked hard to live those teachings. And, to be honest, I found it almost impossible to think and feel only positive thoughts and feelings, especially when the good things I asked for just didn't show up—or did for a moment and then disappeared or showed up, but weren't what I had imagined them to be. I found myself feeling increasingly angry, frustrated, and doubtful of the concepts. I also found myself viewing my own thoughts and feelings as "the enemies," the nemeses of my success. That approach did not work for me at all.

Then I realized that my process was different than that of the authors of those books. My process seemed to be more complex and have more depth. It wasn't just about getting things and experiences I wanted and then defining my life and success by that. My process was about becoming a better person; it was about manifesting the best qualities I, as a human being, could manifest, and then shaping my "askings" from that space. When I did my process my way, my askings were different, and my perception of what showed up was more finely-tuned, and my appreciation was deeper. I felt rich and free of the state of want and lack I had been stuck in. I received more and I shared more. I did *good*—no, I did *God*—wherever I stood. I was manifesting God as I manifested "stuff" on the planet. To quote David Spangler, *"The only successful manifestation is one which brings about a change or growth in consciousness; that is, it has manifested God, or revealed him more fully as well as having manifested a form."*

The idea that all we have to do is decide what we want, ask for it, and then feel good about it until it shows up is appealing. It is tantamount to telling a small child he/she can have anything he/she wants *all the time* just by wishing hard enough. What kid wouldn't love that concept and be totally on-board with that program?

But I ask you: Would it be a good thing for any child to get what he/she wants all the time? Would children always ask or be ready for what they really want? Would they always do good things with that? Would they appreciate it? Would they always ask for things that are healthy and good for them and/or for other people?

Realistically, probably not, because, in addition to all their charming, fun, positive qualities, children are generally immature, emotionally impulsive, mentally under-developed, and pretty self-centered, and sometimes they simply don't care if the things they want aren't good for them and/or could hurt them or other people. They don't have the wisdom yet nor the experience to fine-tune their requests so the results they receive are the most positive, useful manifestations they can produce, for themselves and others. Additionally, children often do not want to have to work or learn or change to arrive at a goal—and as we will discuss later on, work, learning, and change may be the most valuable aspects of manifesting anything.

As adults, we excuse this short-sighted attitude in children. After all, kids are kids. But, the truth is, unfortunately, many adults are still kids in significant ways. We *all* have child-like aspects inside of us alive and well. In some ways, those aspects are beautiful and desirable, but those aspects in other ways, even in fairly "conscious" people, can be pretty *childish*. By childish, I mean immature, self-centered, irrational, and under-developed, especially when compared to our potential or Highest Selves. And, unfortunately, our inner children are often at the core of what we care enough to ask for.

Therein lies the flaw of the New Age Success Teachings. Those teachings make the assumption that we are all conscious, healthy, intelligent, compassionate, mature, wise beings who will only ask for what is good for us and everyone around us, and then use it well. In my opinion, if we are going to learn and master keys to the unlimited power to create whatever we want, we need to simultaneously, and through that process, be seeking and gaining the wisdom, awareness, Heart, and intellect to use that power wisely. That task takes a lot of self-reflection, honesty, and work. We humans, in our childishness, can sometimes be averse to doing all that, unless we see that it will lead us directly to our most desired addictions, toys, and rewards. Thus, the concept that we can have all and everything we want in life is a great carrot to dangle to motivate people to do the challenging Inner Work, but again, in my opinion, this carrot should not be touted as the only, or even primary reason for doing this work.

A mature "success process" will integrate the "magical" New Age Success Teachings with the honesty that any meaningful Human and Spiritual Path calls us to. It will encourage us to maintain an authentic relationship with what is, and our thoughts and feelings about that, while we work to create more of the *goodness*, both inwardly and outwardly, which is really what we want for ourselves and those we love. It will give practical techniques for healing the negative Inner States that seem to take root and grow so naturally when we are presented with life's boogey-men and obstacles—not by denying they exist, but by honestly perceiving, acknowledging, and accepting them, and then calling them *gifts*.

This process will also urge us to find the courage to dig deeply into our darkest pits of fear and despair, and then use the Alchemy of the Heart—our Loving—to transform what we find in those pits into our greatest gold, our truest wealth: understanding, wisdom, compassion, generosity, and kindness, which is our inner richness. We will learn to do our asking from that place, and then this book will encourage us to make that sort of abundance much more available to ourselves, others we are involved with, and ultimately the world. This book is aimed at making all of that realistically simple and practically applicable to you and your life, to the end of loving yourself and others to true success!

SECTION ONE PLAYPAGES

To make it easier for you to understand and utilize the information presented in this book, I'm going to provide PlayPages after Sections One to Three. The worksheets are directions for either written exercises or inner exploration. These exercises will help you discover the truths that exist for you in this material.

Let's begin this process by learning to access our Hearts. This is an important first step. Remember that our Hearts are our connecting points with Spirit and the channels through which the Loving flows through us and into the world. Our Hearts are also the source of our intuitive knowing of what we need to do to fulfill our highest destinies and to create our greatest successes.

Most of us have had experiences of "being in our Hearts." We can use these experiences to create the resource state. By simply remembering previous experiences of being in our Hearts, and then touching a place on our bodies, we can create a physical anchor point, which we can use to access our Hearts and the Loving we experience there, whenever we need that.

Before we do this, I want to reiterate that there are different aspects and qualities of Loving. In creating our resource states and anchor points, we want to make sure we are using experiences that are connected with the Heart Center. Again, for most of us, when we feel "touched" by a person or experience, we naturally refer to the center of our chests to express where this deep contact is taking place. This is the point we want to access for our resource state; this is where we as humans experience the Loving.

Before working with these exercises, please review the information I discussed previously about where the various experiences of loving are seated in the body. In order to effectively access the healing, transformational, and co-creative power of Loving, it is critical that we distinguish between these less evolved aspects of loving and those states of Loving clearly connected to the Heart Center in the middle of the chest. *Choose the experiences and feelings you use for the following exercises carefully.*

EXERCISE ONE
EXERCISE FOR ACCESSING THE HEART
CREATING AN ANCHOR POINT

There are a number of ways we can access our Hearts on a day-to-day basis. One simple strategy follows:

1. Focus on nature, music, a pet, or a baby (whatever works for you). If you feel very emotional or attached to the image you first choose, try something else that touches you deeply but that you feel more neutral about.
2. Identify how this makes you feel. Is the feeling peaceful, harmonious, expansive?
3. Realize that *you are the source of that feeling*—it is coming from within you, not from the external element that triggered it.

4. To claim control and power over this feeling, practice increasing and expanding it. Discover how many different ways you can play with this feeling.
5. Send the feeling to your hands, your feet, any place in your body that feels restricted and that might need love because of hurt, guilt, shame, painful memories, and so on.
6. If you feel you have lost the feeling, which often happens in the beginning, go back to the reference point that triggered it. This is very important, because you will learn that *it is within your power to bring it back.*

It is useful to practice this daily, as a form of meditation, in order to have it become "first nature" for us to go to that place inside of us. I suggest we also create a physical anchor point that we can use to access it. Instructions for that follow:

1. Once you have fully accessed your experience of the Loving energy and are completely present in that state of being, with the fingertip of one index finger touch the place in the middle of your chest where you experience the Loving connection. Simply touch it and be fully present with the Loving, experiencing your Heart for a few minutes. Then, stop touching the point and let go of the feelings and thoughts of Loving. Let the Loving energy stay present with you for as long as it does.
2. Later on, when you are not in your Loving space and you want to be, simply relax and touch that spot in the center of your chest; your anchor point. You will find your Loving space, your connection with your Heart, coming present again.

EXERCISE TWO
LEARNING YOUR WORLDLY TRIGGERS

1. There are other simple ways to increase your awareness of your Heart space. Being with people and in places that allow and encourage you to experience your Heart and your Loving is one. Doing things you enjoy is another. As simple as it sounds, living your life surrounded by that which makes you truly happy is a formula for building your center of joy and Loving. Take a few minutes to list the people, places, and things that help you. As Leo Buscaglia says, "Remember your rapture."
2. Make these people, places, and things an active part of your life.
3. Keep building and adding to your resource state and your anchor point (Exercise One) by using your new experiences with these people, places, and things.

Now that we have had the most basic experience of connecting with our Hearts and using that connection as a tool when we need to, let's take a look at our "stories" about success—and life, money, and the like.

EXERCISE THREE
TELLING YOUR STORY

> "You are the embodiment of the information you choose to accept and act upon. To change your circumstances you need to change your thinking and subsequent actions."
> ~A. Sinclair

OK—let's switch gears here for a bit. Let's begin to explore the origination points of our stories and definitions of wealth and success. I think a very important factor in creating true success is determining our individual beliefs about success, and noting the choices we make based on those beliefs. I think that everyone's core beliefs about success delineate how difficult or easy it is for them to achieve what they call success, and ultimately, determines what success, and failure, look like to them.

So, where do these powerful, yet sometimes disempowering, beliefs come from? My observation after thirty-plus years as a counselor and coach (and sixty-plus years as a human being) is that these beliefs, as well as the related thoughts, feelings, and actions, are born out of watching grown-ups, and the whole world, act out "stories" about money, success, and wealth. We are told and/or determine for ourselves what those stories mean to us and for us before we are even consciously aware of how important the activity of creating success will be to us throughout our lives.

As part of Chapter Three, I shared with you several stories about my childhood/early life experiences with money, wealth, success, and/or the lack of that. Now it is your turn. What are your stories? What did you witness growing up about money and success? What did you see happening with and around money and worldly success when you were a child and teenager? Write it all down. Be detailed and honest.

Then write down the story of what you have done or not done around money and success in your adult life so far, as I did. Take your time. Be thorough.

EXERCISE FOUR
EVALUATING YOUR STORY

Now—read your story. Contemplate it for a while, edit it a bit if it needs that to be an honest representation of what you witnessed as a child, and/or have done for yourself as an adult.

1. Look at your childhood story. Make a list of the "learned" beliefs, assumptions or conclusions you might have made about life, money, and material success from what you witnessed growing up in your family or in the world.

    For example, from what I witnessed as a child and teenager, my beliefs and assumptions might have been that life was full of pain and suffering, especially the work and money aspects of it. I might have learned that the only way to make money was to be greedy, self-serving, and cut-throat. I might have learned that the only alternative to that was to be bitter, angry, and poor. I might have gotten the idea that money is more important than people's well-being, that there was no way to be happy without money—and there was no way to be happy with money.

2. Read through the story you wrote about what you have done around money, wealth, and success as an adult, for yourself. Be honest about ways you might be perpetuating your childhood stories, or using beliefs you formulated from your childhood witnessing (or were consciously taught by grown-ups), even though they may not be working for you. Contemplate it for a while, edit it a bit if it needs that to be an honest representation of what childhood beliefs you have, as an adult, stopped believing or changed, and how that has impacted your adult story.

For example, I decided that work and life could be fun, fulfilling, and rewarding. I taught myself that I could make money being of service and helping people, rather than by conning or hurting them. I learned that I could be happy, feel and share love, help people, do good, have fun and be creative, and that making/receiving money could be a natural, positive end-result of that. I learned that life is good and that the Universe is a loving, friendly, supportive place with more than enough resources and abundance for everyone. I learned that I am a beloved part of all that. This was a very different story than I witnessed in childhood.

Now that we have explored the "stories" we witnessed growing up, and the beliefs we see we have formulated as a result of those stories, and evaluated how we have re-written at least parts of those stories, it is time to do a more detailed examination of what we view as our successes and failures and to redefine them in ways that may be more useful to us.

EXERCISE FIVE
CURRENT SUCCESSES

1. List all the "successes" you have had in your life up until now. These could include being healthy and whole, learning to walk, graduating high school, getting married, having a child, getting the job you want, getting a divorce, buying your dream car, learning to speak up for yourself, overcoming a chronic disease or disability, and so on. They could also include becoming independent of your parents, overcoming your fear of heights, developing a more positive attitude, and so on. Look at your life as it is and write down

anything you deem a success. Be thorough. You might be surprised at how many successes you've had!

2. Categorize the most important of these as either inner or outer success. If an experience seems to span both categories, put it in both. You don't have to do this with every item, unless you want to. This exercise is simply to get you used to looking both inwardly and outwardly for the signs of success.

EXERCISE SIX
REDEFINING FAILURE AS SUCCESS

1. List all the "failures" you have had in your life up until now. These could include anything you honestly look at as unsuccessful events, results, situations, relationships, past, present or future. Look at your life as it stands right now and write down anything that you simply do not feel good about when you look at the outcome; anything that makes you feel small, weak, dissatisfied, victimized or untalented. Then find some kind of success that *is* present in that situation. Sometimes a success may be just "getting through" a negative experience, learning something valuable from it, or heading off in a better direction after it! Play with this exercise; it's yours. Be honest! Be thorough. As Louise Hay comments, "Every experience is a success." Find the success that is or was present in any situation you still hold as a failure inside of you.

2. Categorize the *success* you discovered about those situations as either inner success or outer success.

EXERCISE SEVEN
CLOSED EYE PROCESS
CREATING A "SUCCESS" RESOURCE
STATE AND ANCHOR POINT

Close your eyes. Take some deep breaths. Relax your body by gently tensing your muscles and then relaxing them, in sequence, from your toes to the top of your head and your fingertips. When you are feeling very comfortable, choose one of the successes from your list, and visualize it in your mind's eye. Pick one of the more powerful ones.

Allow the memory of that experience to become fully present. Make sure *you* are part of the memory. See yourself. See everything in great detail—the colors, shapes, foreground and background, other people, whether the picture is clear or fuzzy, bright or dull, in 3-D or flat. Notice where the picture is located in your inner vision.

Pay attention to the sounds associated with that picture. Are they loud or soft, verbal or nonverbal, normal speed or fast or slow? Are they high pitched or low? What is the tempo? Notice whether or not there is a commentary voice—a voice telling you about your picture. Notice where the sounds or voices are coming from and where you hear them.

Next, observe the physical sensations associated with the images of this success. When you watch the picture and hear the sounds associated with it, how does that make you feel physically? Scan your entire body for your visceral sensations.

What are you feeling emotionally when you observe all of this? Really feel the experience again. Let all the wonderful emotional responses from that experience come fully present in you. Live it all over again.

Take a deep breath in and out, and in again. As you inhale this time, allow the whole experience, including the feelings, to get even bigger. As you exhale, allow the scene to stay the same, and as you inhale again, allow it to get even bigger in size, detail, sound, intensity, sensations, feelings, and so on. This process is almost the same as when a balloon increases in size as you blow into it. The image gets bigger as air goes into you. Do this process for several breaths. Adjust the changes occurring in whatever way makes you more comfortable, yet also more empowered. For example, if the increase in sound is annoying, but you like the picture and the feelings bigger, lower the sound and increase the other aspects. You are in control.

The most important part of this is to increase the *feelings* of success, the feelings of victory, accomplishment, empowerment, joy, self-esteem, capability, and so on. These feelings *are* your resource state. The other sensory modalities only serve as a trigger to catapult you into it.

Just before this experience is at its peak, right before you are full to the tippy-top (and more) with the feelings and experience of success, gently, but firmly touch some (other) point on your body that is easily accessible to you, but not often specifically touched by others (like the inside of your knuckle or somewhere on your forearm or your knee). Hold that point while the feeling of success is peaking, then *let it go* as the energy of success begins to dissipate. This spot is your anchor point for your resource state of *success*.

As the state dissipates, gently rouse your body, open your eyes, and begin to move.

EXERCISE EIGHT
FUTURE SUCCESSES

1. Start a list of the areas of your life and selfness which you would like to experience as more successful. Be ruthless and honest with yourself. As Sheldon Kopp reminds us, "If we dare to examine with relentless honesty just how we have been living, we can reshape our lives." Don't go into detail on this, just start your list, and we will talk about what to do with this list later.

SECTION TWO

THE INNER FLOW OF LOVING

CHAPTER FOUR
WHAT IS LOVING?

Rock-and-roll icon, Tina Turner asked us, "What's love got to do with it?" A dying patient of Dr. Bernie Siegal, a pediatric and general surgeon and author of *Peace, Love and Healing*, suggested the answer to that question: "Love is the most important thing in life; nothing else matters. It's all endless love." Wow! Endless love, what a concept! Let's explore it further!

The *American Heritage Dictionary* defines God as, "the perfect, omnipotent, omniscient originator and ruler of the universe; the force, effect or manifestation of this being; Love." It then also offers a definition of love as being "God." So, it would seem that "endless love," as Siegal's dying patient used the phrase, simply defines and is defined as God. In the Bible, this equivalency is made even clearer when in John 4:16, John proclaims, "God is love."

One does not have to look far to find others who agree with this definition of God as Love. Dr. Bertrand Babinet, founder of Babinetics, a system for transforming human consciousness, comments that, for him, God is a place where he feels connected to all things and all people, "A transcendental movement of love." He calls love, "The quintessence of all reality." In *Love Is Letting Go of Fear*, Gerald Jampolsky, concurs when he says, "Love is the only reality there is. Anything that we perceive that does not mirror love is a misperception." Gary Zukav, author of *Seat of the Soul*, agrees, when he writes, "There is nothing but love."

Marianne Williamson, an international lecturer on spirituality and new thought, puts it this way, "Love is the essential existential fact. It is our ultimate reality and our purpose on Earth. Life spent with any other purpose in mind is meaningless, contrary to our nature and, ultimately, painful." Obviously, at least according to all these people, the answer to Tina's famous question is, love has a lot to do with everything.

Some experts, therapists, and doctors specifically focus on the healing power of love. Louise Hay, a therapist who assists people in healing themselves and their lives, contends that "...love is the miracle cure. Loving ourselves works miracles...love is the answer." Joan Borysenko, in her book *Guilt Is the Teacher*, goes even further. She says, "Love is the most basic condition for survival. Love is life force itself. Without it, we would die." Noted psychiatrist Dr. Karl Menninger stated simply, "Love cures. It cures those who give it and those who receive it."

Love is professed by many thoughtful people to be the most powerful force in shaping and influencing many aspects of the human consciousness. Sigmund Freud's writings state that the ability to love is integral to mental and emotional health. Ashley Montagu, anthropologist and author, specifically points to the physical expression of love as a vital key in the development of a whole, healthy human being. M. Scott Peck, author of *A Road Less Traveled*, speaks of love as being necessary to heal a psyche once it has been wounded. Dr. Siegal concurs that love cures both the psyche and the disease. He also states that it cures people, relationships, and lives.

So, what does all of this have to do with us creating more success in our lives? As I have noted, many professionals facilitating personal growth and human health and healing tell us over and over again that love is the energy of the universe. Love is the source of and reason for everything. It creates everything. It heals everything. It is everything. It is God. It is all that is.

If we can understand this concept, not just intellectually, but also viscerally and emotionally, and allow it to become a living reality for us, we can also allow it to empower us to create our truest dreams and most loving visions to be the reality and world we live in every day. So, somewhere in the midst of all that loving are your dreams and mine. Somewhere in the midst of that lies our success. All we have to do is figure out how to access and utilize that loving, that life force, effectively in our consciousness and our lives. The question now becomes, how do we do that?

Each person's process is unique and individual. In the following chapters, I will share my personal experiences, interspersing that with concepts and simple techniques. This will give you a real-life model to relate to—and then the means to apply what this book discusses to your own life.

For me, the beginning of my process of creating myself and my life through the consciousness and with the energy of loving as my guide began with making a choice to "give love a chance" (remember the Beatles song?). I had reached the magical age of twenty-one years. Most of my childhood prior to the age of twelve was pretty much blank. I simply, by unconscious choice, couldn't remember most of it. The rest of my youth, between the ages of twelve and eighteen, seemed like a nightmare to me. The years between eighteen and twenty-one were creative and fun, but not terribly meaningful. Though I knew I did not want to be like my parents, I had not actually decided what I did want to be. I was simply being the most benign person I would have expected myself to be coming out of my horrific beginnings. I was basically "lookin' for love in all the wrong places" (a line from another song, by Waylon Jennings), and in doing that allowed myself to be victimized a lot, and sometimes ended up inadvertently victimizing others. I was, however, smart enough to realize how that pattern, and many others I repeated, would not be effective in creating the life I really wanted for myself and my two kids. I was not living the worst possible life I could have created out of my dismal childhood, but I was also not creating the best possible life I could have envisioned.

Then I read a book called *Autobiography of a Yogi*, by Paramhansa Yogananda. The book touched me. In some ways, of course, Yogananda's process seemed strange and foreign to me; in some ways his experiences were inapplicable to my life. But two pieces of what he discussed impacted me: 1. the purpose and importance of meditation; 2. the idea that I could *choose* to live my life as a Path of the Heart.

I decided right then, in the midst of my arty, "rock-n-roll," drama-filled, twenty-something lifestyle, that the rest of my life would be about following my Heart and discovering a God of Loving inside of me. I hoped that I would then also experience that Loving God in the world and through my relationships. (I think my exact words were: "I've tried sex, drugs and rock-n-roll, and there has to be something more. So, I'm going to go for knowing and experiencing

God. I want to be Love!") I knew intuitively that only that path would allow me to create the life I envisioned.

I want to note here that I am not attached to the word "God" as a name for this Presence, Energy, Force. There are many words in many languages that refer to It. I am simply more familiar with this word than some of the others. I also tend to use words like Spirit, Higher Power, and the Presence. You are free to use whatever words work for you.

I must tell you that the vision I had at the time I chose my path pales beside the reality of living Love that has come forward over my many years of following that path. The wealth I imagined then was nothing compared to the true wealth that now fills my heart and life. But, that original vision was a starting point for me. It motivated me. Intellectually, the idea that Love was the force and essence of everything, that the Universe was essentially not just a friendly place, but indeed stunningly loving did not actually fit my life experience up to that point, nor my concept of reality as I had developed it. But it was what I *really* wanted. So, I went for it!

The idea that everything is in its essence Loving, and that life is meant to be lived as a reflection and expression of that, resonated with an awareness that had surfaced for me when I was very young—pre-orphanage. My parents were fighting—screaming at each other, crying, and hitting each other. It was a scene filled with violence and hurt. Even though I was just a toddler, somehow, I *knew* that the way these people were acting was not the way they were "supposed" to be. I *knew* that the way they were being was not "right." I grabbed onto my mother's skirt and my father's pant leg and tried to pull them apart. I remember screaming and wanting to tell them what I knew—that they should be kind and loving with each other, but I did not have the words to communicate.

As a child and teen, I experienced feeling that way many times as I watched grown-ups' relationships. Later, because of the way the human psyche is programmed by the behaviors it is exposed to as a child, I personally re-enacted mini-versions of the scene I just described many times in my own life and relationships, simply because I didn't know any other way to act. There was always a part of me that knew things could be different, and often I would actually be yelling that Truth in the midst of arguments. I sensed loving could be expressed in every aspect of my relationships and life, but I did not know how to get there.

Yogananda's book affirmed that my instincts were correct and that my life and relationships could be different. He also clarified that first I had to *choose* to do the work it would take to see, feel, be, and experience Loving in every aspect of myself and my life. Then I would have the awareness to learn how to express that Loving through my words and behaviors. The work initially consisted of *connecting* with Spirit, God, the Higher Power, the Loving, through meditation, by choosing to quiet my mind and simply trusting that there was a Loving force that could fill the space created by my silence, and that force could then direct me.

And it did. That force stirred inside of me. It created unrest of a sort. It awakened feelings and memories I did not understand and did not know how to deal with. I realized that this choice, this step I had taken along my path of the Heart to create a life of loving, was just a baby-step.

However, baby-step or not, at the age of twenty-one I had made a powerful choice for someone with a history like mine. I had chosen to explore the possibility that a Loving God and Universe existed and that somehow that presence had something personal and intimate to do with me. I gambled that somehow connecting with that presence, that energy, might change my life for the better. I suspected that this presence cared deeply about me and cared whether or not I created "success," and a life I loved.

As part of that early awakening, I developed a discipline I will continue to practice for the rest of my life. It was a discipline that would allow me to consistently *connect* with that Loving presence, force, energy. I began to meditate. Through meditation first, and later through other experiences in my life, I came to know that the Source energy and all that comprises it, is truly benevolent, kind, loving, abundant, and rich.

At first, I struggled with allowing myself to have and embrace that experience. It conflicted with everything I had known and been taught. But I wanted to shift, heal, release those old beliefs, and I was courageous enough to go for that. As John-Roger, a teacher and friend of mine once said, "It takes great courage to see the Face of God—mostly because first you have to look at yourself."

So, with that thought in mind, what were my next steps? Well, as is somewhat typical of me, I did more research. How did teachers, healers, and esoteric philosophers define and experience Loving?

Tara Singh, author of *A Gift for All Mankind*, notes that, "Everything is created by love." This creative aspect of love is an important one for us to understand. Zukav writes, "Love is not a passive state. *It is an active force.* It is the richness and fullness of your soul flowing through you." John-Roger, and his co-author, Peter McWilliams, in their book, *You Can't Afford the Luxury of a Negative Thought*, reiterates that, "Love is an action." Oscar Ichazo—

founder of the organization, Arica, which teaches integration of the mind, body and emotions—asserts the same belief. Love, in its creative aspect, becomes Loving, a "moving, growing, changing active interplay" between the universe and oneself, oneself and oneself, and oneself and others. Indeed, through the integration of the Highest (Divine) Loving and human beingness, the body and the consciousness become the medium through which the highest spiritual energies can be manifested on the planet as life.

What did the idea of Loving being a *creative* and *active* force mean to me? It meant that I had to participate. Some of what I needed to do was out in the world, but a whole lot of it was inside of me. It involved getting to know honestly who I was and then finding a way to shift that so I could create, promote or allow what I wanted in the world. The way for me to do that was to first see and then love myself in all my many positive and negative aspects. And finally, I had to allow that loving to transform me.

Learning to love myself was the hardest part for me, because I had no reference points for it, and loving myself was an integral step of moving forward on this path I had chosen. Think about it—if a person feels unlovable and/or unworthy, or is filled with negative thoughts and feelings (hurt, anger, shame, guilt, fear, and so on), even if that person takes the time to connect with Spirit and the Loving, they most likely will not let that in. They simply will not feel good enough to receive that powerfully Loving presence into themselves. Receiving the Loving and then filling up with it are necessary next steps to manifesting Loving in the world as our success. The energy of God, of Spirit, is accessible to the human consciousness as Loving. How we perceive ourselves is a huge determinant of the degree to which we can allow this Loving in, which then determines the degree to which we have that energy available to manifest our success in the world.

> "You can start finding Divine Love by loving others, but that doesn't count until you are able to love yourself."
> ~John-Roger

CHAPTER FIVE
WHY LOVING WORKS: THE STRUCTURE OF CONSCIOUSNESS

A friend of mine often says, "The only thing you can really take charge of is the space within your skin." If this is true, then in terms of creating success, it is important to understand exactly what exists within that space. You can learn about the physical aspects from any anatomy book. The aspects which affect your ability to create what you want in your life and to be happy are less understood. A system which I feel explains, simply and effectively, the more intangible elements of being human is the system of psycho-religious thought practiced by the ancient Kahunas of Hawaii.

The Kahunas' system outlines human consciousness in a way that correlates very well with several schools of psychological thought and integrates itself easily, when explored with an open mind, with both Eastern and Western religions. I will neither have nor take the time to explore *all* the possible correlations and integrations between these. I will point out the ones I feel are most relevant, in terms of allowing you to utilize the system to create greater inner and outer success. For more information, please refer to the extensive bibliography at the end of this book.

The origins of the Kahunas' system, which we will call Huna (meaning "secret" in Hawaiian), are lost in preliterate antiquity. However, according to Enid Hoffman, author of *Huna; A Beginner's Guide*, one legend that has been handed down by way of oral tradition is this:

"Long, long ago, when the Sahara Desert was green and fertile, twelve tribes lived in the area. In each tribe there were people who practiced what we would call magic, based on their knowledge of man and nature. When the Sahara Desert gradually dried up and turned to sand, the tribes moved on. They spent some time in the valley of the Nile and helped build the Great Pyramid. They were also involved in the 'mystery schools' of that period.

"The Kahunas had control of their psychic abilities, and those who practiced precognition foresaw a time of darkness coming to Rome. They decided that the tribes needed to move to an area where their beliefs and practices were safe. Using clairvoyance, they saw uninhabited islands in the Pacific, which they chose as their future home. One tribe, for unknown reasons, went instead to the Atlas Mountains of North Africa where some Huna words and practices reportedly survived among Berber tribesmen as late as 1917."

Hoffman continues to discuss the stories of miracles performed by the Kahunas that permeate the folklore of Hawaii. She also notes how Christian missionaries, arriving after 1820, outlawed all practices of the Kahunas. Even today, pious Christians in Hawaii look upon these practices with contempt.

The first non-Hawaiian to investigate the practices of the Kahunas was Dr. William Tufts Brigham, who died in 1921 and was curator of the Bishop Museum of Honolulu. He was friends with the last of the living Kahunas and made notes of the miracles he saw them perform. A man named Max Freedom Long studied with Brigham from 1917 through 1921.

Brigham never really learned the secrets of the Kahunas' "magic," he simply recorded the miracles he observed. Long wanted to understand and, if possible, duplicate, the Kahunas' miracles. In 1934, after much research and contemplation, Long realized that the secrets of the Huna system lay hidden in the native words of the Hawaiian language. By studying the root vocabulary and symbolism of all the words in the Hawaiian dictionary having to do with the mental and spiritual nature of man, he unraveled the mystery.

The information and practices he discovered, when understood and practiced faithfully, can lead not only to healthier, happier human beings, but also to conscious healing of bodies, minds and emotions, as well as circumstances, social tangles, and financial failures. The system itself is simple; the techniques are easy to use. The Kahuna teachings allow us to know exactly how the human psyche works and also to clarify, sort out, and repair parts of it that have not been working effectively. Once the repairs have been made, techniques exist that allow us to create greater success in our lives. The only prerequisites for achieving this more healed and successful state are curiosity, patience, a true willingness to get to know yourself, and profound love and respect for all the parts of yourself you will uncover.

The Kahuna system sees each individual human being as made up of three selves. In Hawaiian, these selves are called "aumakua, uhane, and anihipili." Max Freedom Long called them "high, middle, and low selves." In modern psychology they are often called the superconscious, conscious and subconscious minds. Freud called them the super ego, ego, and id. John-Roger calls them high, conscious, and basic selves. Berne calls them the parent, adult, and child.

Obviously, the concept of humans having three aspects of consciousness living in one body is not new or limited only to the Kahunas. An important differentiation between the Huna and John-Roger's teachings and most of the other systems, is that according to the Kahunas and John-Roger, these are not just parts of our minds. They are actually separate aspects of consciousness or selves.

Each of these aspects of consciousness or selves is very different and unique. It is important that we understand the differences. Following is a brief description; all of this will be covered in greater detail later.

The conscious/middle self is the aspect of us that is conscious, rational, and reasonable. It is the self we are aware of most of the time. It is our inner parent, adult, teacher, and boss. It oversees the low self.

The subconscious/low self is our child self/inner child. It is our physical-emotional beingness. It is irrational, illogical, and fun! It is the seat of our creativity, spontaneity, and joy. It is a wondrous part of our consciousness that is often misunderstood and maligned.

The high self is our "guardian angel." It is a much more highly evolved, aware, and loving aspect of consciousness that watches over the two lower selves. It is wise, all-knowing, and in touch with our higher destiny and purpose. It remembers who we really are.

(For ease of communication, I will simply call the conscious/middle self, the "middle self" from this point forward. I will call the subconscious/low self, the "low self.")

The high self communicates only with and through the low self. It depends on the low self to share this communication with the middle self. The middle self also communicates only with the low self; it has no direct link with the high self. The low self is the critical central piece of a communication network through which the middle self can access higher guidance and direction. This makes for some rather interesting inner dynamics.

Each of the three selves has a consciousness, intelligence, will, and energy body of its own. According to John-Roger, these aspects of consciousness are chosen from repositories of high, middle, and low selves. Each is on its own evolutionary path. Low selves are evolving into middle selves; middle selves are evolving into high selves; high selves evolving into even higher selves. We chose our particular combination of selves in Spirit before birth, in order to manifest both the obstacles we need to go through to learn our life lessons, and the tools and gifts we need to succeed at that to fulfill our destiny.

Max Long used the words middle and low selves for the uhane and unihipili, not to imply that one of these selves is superior to the other, but rather to explain the difference in positioning of these selves in the body. Metaphysically, each aspect of human consciousness relates to a level of the aura or energy field. Each level of this energy field is anchored into the body at a specific physical location.

The levels of the auric field that are related to the middle self are anchored in the head and throat. The auric field related to the low self is anchored mostly in the solar plexus (the third chakra), but it also extends downward into the first and second chakras. (The low self's field of energy also expands upwards to include the

Heart when the low self wants to contact the high self or when it is experiencing being loved.) The center of the field of consciousness called the high self is positioned above and slightly to the right of the physical head (the seventh chakra). This field of energy is anchored in the pineal gland and expresses through the Heart.

Each of the three selves has its own invisible energy body. This body is composed of an etheric (etheric is defined, in physics, as an "all-pervading, infinitely elastic, massless medium, formerly postulated as the medium of propagation of electromagnetic waves"—Webster Dictionary) substance, called "ectoplasm" in metaphysical schools and "aka" in Hawaiian. These energy bodies in Hawaiian are called "kino-aka" bodies (meaning "shadowy bodies"). These bodies are invisible to our physical eyes but can be seen with psychic vision. These three subtle bodies interpenetrate each other and the physical body they use. The aka body of the middle self is multicolored and second in density and size of the three bodies, with the body of the low self being the smallest and most dense.

Each of the three selves uses life force or energy. The low self uses basic life force called "manna" in Hawaiian. The middle self receives life force from the low self and "steps up" the frequency of that for its own use. The life force used by the middle self is called "mana-mana." The high self uses the highest frequency of life force available to us. It is called "Mana-Loa" and comes directly from the universe.

Additionally, the low self sends life force to the high self when it is requesting the creation of something (i.e. in prayer), as an offering, a "sacrifice." The high self then sends that life force, amplified by its own, back to the low self. The low self either uses that life force to physically create what it wants, or it passes the energy along to the middle self, so the middle self can figure out how to manifest the desired creation. We'll discuss more about the ramifications of this arrangement later.

We will be exploring each of the three selves in greater detail in our PlayPages. As we do this, it would be helpful for you to invite the particular self we are discussing to make itself known to you, and for you to notice how it chooses to do that. The exercises at the end of this section can assist you in getting to know and *experience* your selves as fully as possible. The relationship you develop with them, because of this work, will be the key to manifesting all the inner and outer success you could possibly want.

CHAPTER SIX
CONNECTING, RECEIVING AND FILLING UP

"Spirituality for me is recognizing that I am connected to the energy of all creation, that I am a part of it and it is always a part of me." ~Oprah Winfrey

"Love is a force that connects us to every strand of the universe, an unconditional state that characterizes human nature, a form of knowledge (and awareness) that is always there for us—if only we can open ourselves to it." ~Emily H. Sell

Once we have determined that the universe *is* energy-a benevolent, living, healing, nourishing, loving energy-it is then crucial that we understand the importance of connecting to and having a relationship with that energy, and utilizing and shaping that energy in the most positive, creative, healthy way possible within our inner consciousness and our outer lives.

First, we need to understand that there is a natural flow of Loving from unmanifested Spirit to the manifested form. It moves from the objective to the subjective inner reality and then to the outer world. Dr. Bertrand Babinet, in his early healing work, delineated this as the "Movement of the Loving." He determined that this Movement takes place in six steps.

What follows is, basically, my *interpretation* of what he spoke about based on my *experience* of working with his concepts. I have tweaked his system a bit, so that it is more in alignment with my inner process, experience, and awareness. Therefore, I call my explanation the "Flow of Loving," which suits my experience better. There are some differences in how Babinet and I perceive this Flow of Loving, but our essential concepts are similar.

The first three steps represent the internal Flow of Loving—the last three the external. The latter, which we will discuss later in this book, occur somewhat spontaneously, as a result of our choosing to do the first three.

The first of the inner steps is simply "connecting." This step involves connecting to one's spiritual energy, Soul, God, or Source of Love, however one perceives that, in whatever ways are appropriate and work for each individual. (There are several ways to do this, varying for individuals. A few are meditation, contemplation, and prayer.) Connecting allows us to access the flow of Loving Energy, like connecting a hose to a running faucet might allow one to access the water. Connecting allows us to access the living pool of neutral Loving that simply *is* the energy of the universe, waiting to be put to good use. Choosing to tap into this Source energy, identifying with it as one's own Source energy, and then choosing to make that a priority in one's life, as I did at the age of twenty-one, is the beginning of any path about creating a life in alignment with Spirit and one's own spiritual beingness, the Soul. It is the core of building one's inner sense of self and one's outwardly manifesting life based on and filled with this Loving presence that *is* the Source material and state of the universe.

The second step is "receiving." Receiving allows this flow of Loving, the energy of the universe, God/Love, to move into us; we simply let it in. This is a position of surrender and trust, of receptivity and openness. It is a position of permitting. We permit Spirit to "feed" us, to suckle us at the breast of a tender, compassionate, and abundant Mother-God. This is the step where we can see that our personal issues about ourselves and our worthiness can get in the way; those issues can block the flow of the Loving.

The third step in the inner flow is called "nurturing." Nurturing is simply filling ourselves up with the God energy. This is a step many individuals have great difficulty taking. Even if we have been courageous enough to choose to connect, and even if we love ourselves enough to let ourselves receive the Loving presence of the universe, we tend to want to "give away" the Loving as soon as we receive it, as soon as it comes in. We allow it only to pass through us, without allowing it, first, to heal and nourish us. Nurturing is simply "filling our own cup" first. It is allowing ourselves to become whole, healthy, happy human beings. It is self-loving.

Nurturing and caring for ourselves until we are satiated with our own loving and through that, the Loving of the Universe, is important. Out of this fullness will quite naturally come the Flow of Loving out into the world. So, first, we connect and receive the Loving, the life force from God or Spirit—the simple Goodness that is—then, we allow that to fill us up, heal, inspire, and nourish us, and, finally, we share that, as loving, with others.

It is important, in the beginning, that we use the Loving, in its healing capacity, to transform the vehicle through which that energy flows on its trip into the outer world, so that it can then manifest with integrity in its creative mode. That vehicle is *us*—our beingness on all levels. This is the "growth or change in consciousness" that can come forward through the process of successful manifestation. If our consciousness—who we are as people—is healthy, rich, happy, and full of Loving, our outer manifestations, our creations, our lives, and relationships will reflect that. If our consciousness is unhealthy, poor, miserable, twisted, and dark, our relationships, our lives, our creations will also reflect that.

So, if Loving is the energy of the universe, why aren't we all automatically connected to and filled up with it? Why don't we consciously experience being loved? Why does it often seem so difficult to be Loving?

To answer those questions, I need to refer you to the structure of human consciousness outlined in Chapter Five. Then I need to delineate a bit more detail. If later you want more information and details, you can read Long's books.

The low self is the aspect of our psyche that closely correlates to what psychologists call the inner child. It is present as us when we are born. It grows and develops until it reaches its fullness, at about the age of five or six years. It has its own basic nature, but essentially it is shaped by our early life experiences, and the ways our parents and other grown-ups interact with it, through what they say to it, the way they treat us as children, and through what they teach us about life. *And*, simultaneously, those adults are teaching and shaping the aspects of our consciousnesses that will later become our middle selves—our adult selves.

The middle self is a blank when one is born, though certain genetic tendencies will be built in, waiting to be activated. For the most part, our middle self is developed by watching and listening to the grown-ups around us. As a result of that interaction, the relationship between a person's low self and their middle self is very similar to what a child's relationship was with his/her parents. Also, essentially, the middle self is the primary shaper of our life paradigm as we mature.

The high self is not very involved with this shaping process, even though it holds the blueprint for what we are meant to do and be in our life. Although the low self is very connected to the high self at or around birth, a veil drops on that relationship when a child is around eight, when development of the middle self takes priority. So, though bits and pieces of information transmitted by the high self to the low self will be communicated clearly to the middle self, most of it is lost, until such time as the middle self/adult person decides to reconnect with the high self. Then, to effectively reconnect with their spiritual self, a person will need to understand and work effectively with their low self, or inner child.

Now, what is clear to me through perceiving this inner dynamic going on in each human being, is that there is lots of opportunity for information to get garbled, and for one aspect of self to have a totally different agenda than the others. Also, wounds and distortions in one part of oneself can inflict upon and interfere with the intentions of other aspects of self. Also, for one's consciousness, and thus one's creative process and success mechanism to work most effectively, all these aspects of self need to be clear and aligned with one's purpose/intention/vision/askings.

As Alfred Adler commented, "All human failures are the result of lack of love." We might also say that all human success is the result (or end-product) of Loving. Accessing Loving, becoming Loving, and expressing that clearly can be a key to achieving greater success within ourselves and on the planet. Love is the substance from whence all success is shaped, and loving is how we shape it. Loving, indeed, becomes the Heart of our success.

CHAPTER SEVEN
THE POWER OF SELF-LOVING

> "Wouldn't it be powerful if you fell in love with yourself so deeply that you would do just about anything if you knew it would make you happy? This is precisely how much Life loves you and wants you to nurture yourself. The deeper you love yourself, the more the Universe will affirm your worth. Then you can enjoy a lifelong love affair that brings you the richest fulfillment from inside out." ~Alan Cohen

Many people have negative perceptions about self-love. I see loving ourselves as next to loving God/Spirit in importance. I feel that each of us needs to have, securely anchored and harbored inside of us, the experience of being loved, which we can then share with others. As we mature, a huge aspect of that is, of course, connecting to the Loving of Spirit. Perhaps an even more empowering aspect of the experience of being loved is derived through loving ourselves. Loving ourselves allows us to have a reference point for experiencing a universal energy of Loving/Divine Love, as well as the Loving of other human beings in our world. Frankly, it is my experience that if a person does not love themselves, it is difficult for them to perceive the Universe or God as a Loving place or Source. It is also difficult for them to experience that other people love them, or even that loving is simply present in the world; that the world is a safe and loving place.

Ideally, people will have experienced being loved by their parents as children. But often that loving is flawed and/or unhealthy, and sometimes, it is even non-existent. As a result, many people grow up lacking the stable, solid inner experience of being loved. Then, because in our psyche our experience of God is often colored by our experiences of our parents, who were seen as Gods by us in our child-minds and worlds, we become afraid or doubting when it comes to believing that there is a force or power in the universe that loves us fully and completely. So, it is difficult to trust it and to open to it.

The only way to shift that is to give ourselves a solid, stable, healthy, unconditional, trustworthy model of loving through the way we love ourselves. Then we become capable of conceiving of and experiencing a Loving God—and, as a result of that, we become capable of extending that loving to others in healthy ways. I believe that when we find an effective balance between loving ourselves and loving others, between being loved and being loving, we are more able to promote and create our highest and best needs and wants in our lives, rather than obsessively focusing on baser ones. Why? Simply because we are always *full* inside, and thus not creating from a place of lack—an existence in which we are simply hungry, unsatisfied souls.

In his book, *The Faces of Love*, John B. Terbough notes that much unhappiness is related to improper love of self. He writes, "If we truly love ourselves as we should, we will always put the Soul's interests before those of the body." I would add that treating our body and our human consciousness with kindness and compassion is essential for fulfilling the "Soul's interests." Loving our humanness allows the body, mind, emotions, and imagination to be more effective and more willing vehicles for God's joy, love, laughter, peace, and abundance. We'll discuss this relationship again as we move forward, but, rest assured, there is no disparity between the form of Loving that fulfills one's highest purpose and the form of loving that fulfills one's responsibility to the body and consciousness here. The inner and outer realities do relate and can "match" and be balanced.

So how does this all work utilizing both Max Freedom Long's description of the structure of human consciousness and the basic model of the Movement or Flow of Loving? Let's start by playing with these concepts a bit and perhaps giving ourselves an experience of the most natural and effective way the energy of the Universe, the energy of Loving, flows through us as us.

SECTION TWO PLAYPAGES

Recognizing each of the three selves and their differences is important if we are to encourage more communication between them. These PlayPages will get you started on this process. I recommend keeping a journal of your experiences with the three selves, so you can measure your progress and track your results as you move through these exercises.

Of the three selves, the middle self is the easiest to recognize because we live in its awareness most of the time. Generally speaking, if we observe our thoughts, perceptions, and beliefs, we can get a good idea of our middle self's nature. A really simple exercise to do to gain this familiarity follows:

EXERCISE ONE
GETTING TO KNOW THE MIDDLE SELF

1. Look at a current life situation.
2. Observe your *obvious* experience of it. What is your most *conscious* perception of what is going on, both in the environment and within yourself? What do you *think* about

the situation? What do you *think you feel* about it? What are your judgments and observations? Simply put, what are your thoughts? What is in your mind?

3. Take note of these in your journal.

These observations reflect your middle self and your middle self's perceptions of this situation. The low and high selves and their viewpoints are a bit more difficult to access. Because of this, we will approach them through a kind of "back door"—that is, by experiencing them in contrast to the middle self. Let's start by differentiating between the two lower selves. Here's a visualization that will allow you to get to know each of them better:

EXERCISE TWO
CLOSED EYE PROCESS
MIDDLE SELF/LOW SELF VISUALIZATION

(The closed eye processes in this book are easier to do if you first read the guided visualizations into a tape recorder as though you were leading someone else through them. Then, making yourself comfortable, play the tape back, allowing it to lead you through the exercise.)

Close your eyes and make your body comfortable. Breathe deeply several times. Relax your body by gently tensing your muscles and then relaxing them, in sequence, from your toes to the top of your head and your fingertips. Then, let go of any disturbing thoughts or feelings by breathing into them and releasing them as you exhale. Continue this process until you feel completely relaxed.

Once your body, mind, and emotions are at ease, *close your eyes* and go inside. Imagine a movie screen that sits just behind your eyelids and slightly above your physical line of vision. Invite your middle self to come to you as a vision on this screen. Mentally review some of the notes you've made about your conscious thoughts, beliefs, perceptions, and approaches in various life situations. Out of that, allow a deepening sense of who and what your middle self is to be more fully present with you.

Once you feel and sense the middle self, allow a vision of that self to come onto your screen. Let that vision be your middle self representing itself to you. Receive and welcome it to you. Observe it. Notice all of its characteristics, positive and not so positive. Talk with it. Ask your middle self its name; ask it to tell you about itself. Listen carefully. Notice the quality and tone of the middle self's communication.

When you feel comfortable with your middle self, notice the environment around it. This is your middle self's home. See, feel, and hear the details of this environment. Realize that everything you perceive is an expression, a representation of your middle self. Take it all in. Get to know this part of you better. Take your time. Let it become familiar.

Now, even though you are viewing this scene and your middle self on the screen of your imagination, let yourself become part of the picture. Begin to come fully present with this self in its environment the same way you would if you were engrossed in watching a movie. Be on the screen, participating, while you are observing the picture. See, feel, and hear everything as though you were there, on the screen with the middle self.

Once you feel totally involved, notice a path leading off into the distance. Notice the path twisting and winding until it comes to a bridge spanning a stream of pure crystalline water. Hear the melodious music of the water.

Observe that on the other side of the bridge the environment appears to be very natural and earthy. You can almost smell the moist dirt and the grasses and flowers. Listen to the soft sounds of birds. The wind is calling to you through the trees. You know you must follow this path.

Say goodbye to your middle self for now. Let it know you will be back. Ask it to wait for you by the bridge until you return. Begin to walk down the path.

Feel the texture of the path beneath your feet. Notice the twists and turns of the path as you follow it. It disappears into a thickly wooded area. The environment becomes darker and more mysterious...curiouser and curiouser, as you walk deeper and deeper into the forest. At times you feel hesitant about going farther, but each time you think of stopping and going back, you discover a treasure: a radiant crystalline rock formation, a fragrant flower, a butterfly, or a leaf. You continue on, deeper and deeper-- delighted, entranced, and curious.

And then, suddenly, you find yourself in a clearing. You stop and gaze around you; there is a mystical, magical quality to everything you see—the wildflowers scattered everywhere in radiant colors, the gentle creatures feeding on the tender grasses of the clearing, the brilliant sunlight streaming down on the swaying branches of trees at the periphery. Everything is quite beautiful.

You notice a large moss-covered rock slightly hidden under the arching branches of a tree off to your right. You walk closer to it. Perched on the rock, hidden in the branches, is another being. This one is a pure and innocent creature of the earth—an elemental, a child-like creature. There something magical and special, and very real, open, and honest about this creature. Observe its appearance, the qualities of its movements, and any sounds it makes.

Notice that even though the being is, perhaps, a little shy and hesitant about making contact with you, all its feelings and thoughts are revealed to you through its expressions and movements. Quietly, you begin to talk to this creature, gently inviting it to respond to you. You notice its features and the qualities of its form as you talk.

As the being answers your questions and begins to shape itself with you, you feel its beingness moving deeply within you. A profound, natural knowing springs forward inside of you. A sense of kinship develops; *you know this being*. You realize it is your low self.

You are *very* curious about it. You spend more time talking with it and sharing, noticing everything. You ask lots of questions; questions that let you get to know it better. You learn its name, its age, chat about what kinds of things it likes or doesn't like, and how it feels about its existence. It answers you clearly, though, at times, hesitantly. You are touched and deeply enchanted. You stay with this being for as long as you can, and then, you know it's time to go.

You invite your low self to walk back with you to the edge of the forest, to the bridge. If it agrees to go with you, take it by the hand and walk with it, taking your time and walking as quickly as you and your low self wish. If your low self chooses not to go with you today, lovingly say goodbye to it at the rock, and let it know you will return soon to spend time with it.

Walk back to the bridge. Let yourself move to a quiet, peaceful state of aware awakening. Gently move your body in comfortable ways. Take several deep breaths. Bring yourself present, here and now.

EXERCISE THREE
CLOSED EYE PROCESS
MIDDLE SELF/LOW SELF COMMUNICATION

(This exercise should only be done when the low self is ready to leave the rock and walk to the bridge with you. For most people this will mean doing Exercise One several times. Once the low self feels comfortable leaving the rock to walk with you, continue the above visualization as follows:)

Walk with your low self, holding its hand, to the edge of the forest and to the bridge. Take the time to look around you and share this location with the low self. It may have never been here before. Notice the peacefulness and beauty of this area. Listen again to the gentle song of the water and the birds. Observe the lush green vegetation and the delicate flowers. Invite your low self to drink of the natural beauty and peace around you.

As you approach the bridge, notice that your middle self is still waiting for you. Ask your low self if it would like to meet the middle self. If it agrees, take it by the hand and lead the way. Beckon to the middle self to meet you halfway, at the center of the bridge.

When the three of you come together on the bridge, introduce the low self to the middle self. It's possible that they've already met. Be sensitive to any signs that they have interacted before and notice whether that previous contact appears to have been positive, or not. If there is hesitation or ill-feelings, encourage the two selves to talk to and through you about their feelings. Have them share their thoughts and perceptions of their previous experiences. Stay with them, gently leading them in their conversation, until they feel comfortable talking with each other. Encourage them, lovingly, to work out their sensitive areas and to talk and listen to each other.

Allow them to communicate their honest points of view, while maintaining the *safety* of the situation and *respect* for each self. Teach them to do that for themselves if they don't already know how.

Once the conversation has developed to a place where the two selves are comfortable talking together, let them know it is time for you to leave. Encourage them to continue their conversation, for as long as and in whatever ways would be beneficial for them. If either of them doesn't feel comfortable without you just now, reassure them that that is OK; that you will come back often go help them work out their difficulties and forge a new relationship.

Before leaving, and regardless of the status of their relationship, have them establish a way to "call" to each other when they want to meet again. Then let them each go to their own homes, or to continue talking with each other, whichever they prefer.

Begin moving out of your imagination. Let yourself again simply be an observer. Gradually, let the images on the screen begin to fade, until they are gone. Bring yourself back to a quiet, peaceful state of aware awakening. Gently move your body in comfortable ways. Take several deep breaths. Find yourself in the present here and now.

Write in your journal after these exercises. Note any differences you perceive between the middle self and the low self. In your visualization, they presented themselves to you in a "physical" form, spoke to you in an "audible" voice, and interacted with you through a "personality." What were these like? They represent aspects of that self's beingness.

Additionally, observe where in your real-life body you experienced each consciousness, what each of them felt like, and the differences in your state or viewpoint while you were relating to them; differences you may have noticed physically, emotionally or mentally. Also, note variances in the tone, quality, and content of any communication you received from either self. This is important information and will be helpful later.

Getting to know all our selves is important. Getting to know our low selves is especially critical. Remember, the low self acts as a liaison between the middle and the high selves. It is an integral link in our inner communication network; a link which can be complex and difficult to understand.

The low self is our *subconscious mind*; that is, it lives just beneath our normal, waking level of awareness. It can be very challenging for us to communicate with. The low self's messages, and its means of conveying them can be very subtle and, often, somewhat cryptic and symbolic—at least, to the middle self.

Deciphering the low self's communiqués becomes an even more complex process when we realize that it is possible for an individual to have more than one low self. Each of these separate low selves has a different "personality," a consciousness all its own. Each self can be either male or female, and none of them needs to be the same sex as the physical body. This can result in a wide range of possible variances that make it difficult for individuals to access clear, useful information from the low self.

The most effective approach to dealing with multiple or different-sex low selves is simply to love them and the situation inside of you, rather than entering into judgment. If we *accept* the challenge of assisting our low selves in understanding each other, and in communicating with the middle self, we find they move into a state of cooperation very quickly. It is definitely worth our time and trouble to accept this challenge, because until our low selves are cooperating with each other and the middle self, our lives will be, to say the least, very *interesting*!

(NOTE: More than one middle self is unlikely, although, in some cases, mental illness may be the result of such an anomaly. Middle selves are also usually, but not always, the "same sex" as the physical body. High selves are a "two acting as one" consciousness, having both a masculine and a feminine aspect, but still functioning as one, somewhat "unisex" consciousness.)

Keep all of this in mind as we solicit and track information from the low self (or selves). It may take a while to sort everything out. Not all low selves are willing to reveal themselves right away and, sometimes, multiple low selves may be difficult to distinguish. As we embark on this path of self-discovery, be patient and open to whatever you find.

Before we work and play any more with the middle and low selves, let's lay the groundwork for our relationship with the high self, and, through that, Spirit. This relationship will be our access point for spiritual guidance and energy.

EXERCISE FOUR
A PLAYFUL WAY TO GET TO KNOW LOW SELF

MATERIALS: Large sheets of plain paper and crayons or markers; a journal separated into separate areas for low, middle, and high self notes

1. Close your eyes. Do some gentle relaxation. Then, go back inside to that place where, in our previous visualization, you met with your low self/inner child. Spend some time visiting with it.

2. Open your eyes. Keeping the presence of the low self with you, draw a picture of it. Take your time and relax. Let your low self guide you. Let the picture unfold from inside you, not from your mind, but from your Heart and from your memory of this being, and from the being itself.
3. When the picture is finished, spend some time studying it. How do you feel about this picture? What is it saying to you? What does it show you about your low self?
4. Let your low self write about this picture at the bottom of the page, if it feels so inclined. Date the picture and keep it in a folder for later reference.
5. Have the middle self write in the journal about its experience of this exercise.

EXERCISE FIVE
ANOTHER WAY TO COMMUNICATE WITH THE LOW SELF

MATERIALS: Pen and paper; your journal

1. Close your eyes. Do some gentle relaxation. Go again to the clearing where you communed with the inner child/low self. Have the picture you drew in the last exercise available as a resource.
2. Open your eyes. Have your middle self write a letter to the low self, inviting it to tell the middle self all about itself. Be sure to set up a tone of trust, safety, acceptance, honesty, respect, and loving. Let the low self know that, whatever your history has been, you (as a middle self) are committed to creating a kind, loving relationship with it. Emphasize that if you are to succeed in doing this, you need to know more about the low self. Once this understanding has been

established, have the middle self write out questions that invite the low self to reveal itself more fully.
3. Have the low self respond on a separate sheet of paper or in its own designated area of your journal. Allow the low self to answer the questions in any way that's appropriate for it. It can draw pictures or write out words. Remember the low self operates at the level of a young child. Appreciate that. Be patient.
4. Once the low self has finished, have the middle self review the low self's sharings. Be sure the middle self pays attention to the information it is receiving. Then, when this communication feels complete, have the middle self thank the low self for sharing with you.
5. Be sure to have the middle self make notes in its part of your journal, of its experience of communicating with the low self.

Remember to thank the low self after each of its communications. Many low selves, like children conversing with an adult, do not feel safe. This is especially true if the middle self has, in the past, been critical, rejecting or abusive. The fact that low selves will talk to us at all, after some of the treatment they have received, is a miracle. We need to acknowledge that and express our appreciation.

EXERCISE SIX
CONNECTING TO THE HIGH SELF
CLOSED EYE PROCESS

The relationship between the high and low selves—and the energy of Loving and Spirit that comes through that—can add sweetness to our inner environment. The wisdom, knowing, and practical guidance the high self shares with the middle self, via the low self, can enhance our abilities to create abundantly in the world. A healthy, happy, cooperative relationship between the two lower selves can serve as the core of our inner success.

In the words of Max Long, "Under normal conditions the union between the low and middle selves can be made a very satisfactory matter." It can become a near perfect example of cooperation and interdependence. Under abnormal conditions, when the low self is denied its proper share of focus and attention, and when its natural needs and desires are disregarded over a long period of time, an unrecognized war between the two selves takes place. Lack of harmony engenders lack of health (and, ultimately, lack of success and abundance). It is very foolish to follow a mode of life which makes it impossible for the two selves to live together in harmony.

For the utmost in normal, happy living, the high self must also be given its proper part and place in life. When this is done and there is harmony and closeness in the relationship between the three selves, conditions are at their very best for creating true success on every level.

EXERCISE SEVEN
CLOSED EYE PROCESS
THREE SELF VISUALIZATIONS
PUTTING IT ALL TOGETHER

Close your eyes. Take some deep breaths. Relax your body by gently tensing your muscles and then relaxing them, in sequence, from your toes to the top of your head and your fingertips. If you have any disturbing thoughts or feelings, just inhale into the areas of your body or mind in which they are located, and when you exhale, release them with the breath.

Once you have relaxed fully and feel very comfortable, go inside, visualizing the place where you met previously with your middle self. Bring the middle self present. Converse for a bit. Suggest that it is time for the middle self to encourage the low self to contact and communicate with the high self. Ask the middle self to review, for its own information, all the reasons why this contact is valuable and how the low self can benefit from it also. Then instruct the middle self to call to the low self in whatever way they have established. Have them meet at the bridge.

When the low self arrives, observe the qualities of loving, compassion, peace, acceptance, and trust that are now present between these two selves. As the middle self instructs the low self to contact the high self, note the quiet sense of authority with which the middle self communicates and the sense of trust with which the low self listens. Notice also the mutual respect which is present between them. As the middle self completes its instructions on exactly how the low self should contact the high self, it promises the low self that it will wait by the bridge while the low self returns to its clearing to fulfill its task of contacting the high self.

As the low self returns to the clearing, watch as it quietly assumes a sitting position by its mossy rock. Observe as the low self closes its eyes and begins to breathe deeply. It inhales into its belly, raising the abdomen visibly. Then it exhales deeply into all of its body and into the universe. It does this again and again, at least three times (more as needed). Then, when it is prepared and in a state of peace, the low self inhales deeply and exhales, opening its arms and Heart and turning its face and beingness skyward, sharing the loving and fullness of its beingness...surrendering it to the Great Parent Spirit that awaits. After a few minutes of sharing itself like this, the low self returns to normal breathing and a quiet, eyes-closed position, waiting.

Very soon you notice a powerful mist, a sparkling, swirling cloud descending from the sky, forming near the rock and your low self. A being is shaping itself out of this mist. Observe this being with all your inner senses. What does it look like, feel like, sound like, even smell and taste like? Notice a radiant light that penetrates the body of this Being and extends away from it for some distance.

Watch as this Light extends to surround and enfold the low self. Sense the communion they become involved in; the deep, nonverbal exchange that is taking place between them. Loving passes between them as Light. The low self relaxes even more and with a satisfied sigh, opens more to receive the Loving and the Light. The high self fills and surrounds the low self with this Loving energy. The high self extends knowing and awareness through this Loving to the low self. It gives guidance and advice in an unspoken language of feelings, images, and subtle sensations that are understood perfectly by the low self. Watch as the low self fills and fills again with this Beingness, this Knowingness, this Love.

Watch as it overflows and then watch as it relaxes, opening to receive more...and watch as the high self gives again, even more. Feel and sense this exchange within you. Partake of its glory and its pleasures. Receive of the Loving.

As this interaction completes itself, notice the high self again becoming a nebulous cloud of sparkling mist...drifting upwards and away, until it disappears. Notice a wispy thread of Light still stretching between the dissipating mist floating Heavenward and the Heart of the low self, who is still deep in a state of communion.

And then the mist is gone. The low self slowly awakens. Its eyes open, still seeing or perceiving that which is beyond words. The low self sits for a while and then arises and returns to the bridge, where the middle self has been patiently waiting.

The middle self asks to know what the high self shared. The low self, using pictures, body sensations, feelings, and some words, now all very familiar to the middle self, translates and communicates the Loving, warmth and wisdom of the high self. The middle self receives of this, understanding it perfectly, and then gives thanks to the low self. Now friends and lovers, the two selves say goodbye to each other and return to their own worlds to continue fulfilling their functions and tasks perfectly, even better now that the high self has blessed them with its Loving input and its presence.

You are moved deeply by the experience you've just shared with them. You feel safe and comfortable knowing these beings and their relationships are developing. You sense that your entire life is being enhanced by this clear, frequent, and loving communication. Your fate and destiny are in compassionate and competent hands—hands that are indeed your own—hands that belong to your three selves.

In the stillness of your Heart, as you feel complete with this exercise, begin to gently move your body. Take several deep breaths. Open your eyes. Find yourself here and now.

We have discussed the Inner Flow of the Loving—connecting, receiving, and filling up—in previous chapters. The Outer Flow of the Loving—expressing and envisioning, practical reasoning/planning, and action—will be outlined in the last three chapters.

But first, let's explore how these two explanations work together perfectly to show us how the human psyche is constructed to interface perfectly with Spirit and to act as a conduit for the energy of the Universe, and how that can assist us in creating that which we call success.

EXERCISE EIGHT
A CLOSED EYE PROCESS
THE FLOW OF THE LOVING

Close your eyes and make your body comfortable. Breathe deeply. Relax your body, using the techniques described in the earlier exercises. When you are relaxed and comfortable, begin the process.

Moving to that place inside of you that you are beginning to know as your Heart, invite the energy of Spirit, the Loving, to come more fully present within you. Be soft and open to it.

Visualize this Loving coming through you as a gentle stream of golden Loving Light moving to you from somewhere in all the universes, from the Source of Love and Light. This stream of Love is gently connecting with you through the top of your head, easing its way into your body. It moves as a flowing stream of Light toward your Heart. It touches it and begins to fill your Heart with its warm, soothing, healing Loving. Your Heart fills with this energy, welcoming it and receiving it. Your Heart expands and stretches its parameters to receive more. Your Heart feels full to overflowing, almost as though it could burst. Then you notice a warm stream of this golden energy trickling from the fullness of your Heart into your body...down your arms...into your torso...filling your legs...then upwards to your neck and throat...and finally into your head. Soon your whole body is full of this Light, Loving energy.

All of you is being soothed and comforted and filled. Notice that you feel abundant. You must *stretch* yourself to receive all of the Light and Loving moving into and through you.

Just when you feel so full that you might burst, you notice this Light energy extending beyond your body, expanding outward as a radiance. You especially notice pools of this energy around your hands, mouth and eyes, waiting to be shared, and urging you to share. You notice, as you look out into the world from this fullness, that you see people and circumstances that need this energy. You know intuitively, and from your wisdom and experience, the most effective ways to move this Light and Loving into these situations to produce the most powerful and poignant results. You do this. You see it happening.

You realize this energy is endless. As you share it and utilize it to do good work, more comes to you. The stream of energy continues to pour into you, filling you, and you continue to receive it, filling up with it. It continues to overflow and move out into the world. From that Source inside of you, and from your own wisdom and experience, you continue to know where to use it and how to produce the best results.

Then you begin to notice that from the world—from these people and situations and others—you are being offered an abundance of loving, and "the world." You receive it gratefully, using it appropriately, as you want and need, giving away that which is not for you and giving of the overflow again. In "great-fullness," you turn again to the Source of the Loving and give thanks from your Heart and find again the stream of Loving moving into you even more.

As you relax and enjoy this cycle of Loving and abundance you notice various current situations in your own life being touched by this Loving and being healed, made whole and better. Success becomes a natural and obvious aspect of your life and vision, because the success, abundance, and fullness are already present inside of you, easily and effortlessly. They manifest fully in every situation and relationship you find yourself in.

Enjoy and savor your success. When you are ready, bring yourself back to the present moment. Gently rouse your body and open your eyes. Bring the fullness of this exercise with you as you move out into the world.

Remember, you are a winner when you have a life you love. Don't stop short of that! Follow the flow of the Loving through all the ins and outs of your human beingness, straight to your success!

SECTION THREE

THE PRACTICE OF LOVING

CHAPTER EIGHT
FORGIVENESS

> "The basic thing we need to do is to forgive ourselves for forgetting that we are divine. That is the real message (we need to hear) to open up the channel for our return to Spirit (and for Spirit to assist us in our lives)." ~John-Roger

Throughout this book, a lot of emphasis has been placed on connecting with Spirit. Spirit is the Source of our Loving, and Loving is the source of our success. The first step in the flow of the Loving from Spirit to manifested form is "connecting." The low self must connect with Spirit, through the high self, before we can receive the bounty and blessings that are ours—the abundance that constitutes our spiritual heritage.

Much of the work and play we have done in earlier sections has been designed to assist us in creating a relationship between our middle and low selves that allows and inspires us to make this higher connection, and then to do our "asking" from the healthiest, most loving place inside of us. And yet, even once we think we have succeeded in becoming happier, healthier, more loving, peaceful and integrated human beings, many of us still do not manage to access our Divine heritage/resources. We still do not claim our birthright as spiritual beings. We do not do our asking from a state of or an expectation of Grace. (Grace here is being defined as favor/gifts bestowed freely upon us by Spirit, simply because it is the nature of God/Spirit/the Universe, to be rich, Loving, and giving.) We do not experience that Spirit is our partner in life here on Earth. Why?

Most of us don't claim our innate sense of wealth, our inner riches, nor do we experience our worldly successes as coming from/through collaboration with Spirit, simply because we judge ourselves as unworthy of that. In doing so, we separate ourselves from all that could be ours both inwardly and outwardly, through Spirit, because we don't feel we deserve it and we think we are not "good enough."

Certainly, the shifts we have made in our inner relationships (between the selves) can help us to overcome this basic block to manifesting our "structurally-ordained" connection to Spirit (through our high selves), but there is more we can do. Indeed, there is more we *must* do if we are to claim who we are: children of the Highest God, the God of Loving. The "more" we must do consists of three simple but important processes, all of which encourage the greater presence of Spirit, the high self and Loving in our lives, by allowing us to affirm to ourselves that we are "good enough." These processes are forgiveness, gratitude, and service and they work with clearing negative emotions and beliefs in the low self at a very deep level. They also work with realigning the middle self's perceptions and beliefs about behaviors and actions we or others may have perpetrated here.

The first of these processes is forgiveness. In his most recent book, *Forgiveness*, John-Roger notes that forgiveness is "the key to the kingdom. It not only opens the door, it's the hinges on the door, it's the key to the door, and it's also the little bell that rings and lets you know the door opened." Despite this testimony to the seemingly inherent importance of the act of forgiveness, in the foreword of the same book, Paul Kaye comments honestly that "forgiving...certainly seems to go against the grain of our human conditioning." I would tend to agree.

Many of us see forgiveness as being contrary to our natural learning process. We believe that if we do not note and remember our errors (and hold them against ourselves), we will not learn from them. We also believe that if we do not note and remember the offending actions of others (and hold those against both them *and ourselves*), we will allow those others to hurt us again, thus making the same mistake twice, which is often judged as being "stupid."

This basic concept of learning is flawed. It assumes we are here to learn how not to make mistakes, how to do whatever we do *perfectly*. In actuality, all we are here to learn is to love ourselves, others, and everything "as is." And, according to Jesus, John-Roger, and many other spiritual teachers, "Love is forgiving."

True forgiveness is often seen as an action of weakness. It is seen as the attitude of a "sucker" and a "wimp." Yet Jesus spoke constantly of forgiveness as the means of "entering the kingdom of Heaven"—a kingdom which, according to the Kahuna teachings, is accessible to us only through the high self. Seconding this, John-Roger notes that in practicing forgiveness, we become "commutators of Divine energy into this world, and the kingdom of Heaven as it appears in us, around us, as us."

Interestingly, as we have read in previous chapters and experienced through the exercises in the PlayPages, it is the low self's job to connect with the high self. And, it is the low self that the middle self most often judges. So, it becomes obvious that the most powerful aspect of forgiveness that needs to take place is forgiveness of the low self by the middle self—and vice versa. Then, as those very human aspects of self come into harmony and alignment, the middle self can and will direct the low self to connect with that higher source of energy, guidance, and wisdom that is always available to every human being through the high self. Both aspects of personal self will feel and believe they are worthy of such a connection.

Clearly, through forgiveness, it becomes our destinies to receive the energy of Loving with all our human beingness, and to share that with the world as we are directed through our Loving Hearts. To my way of thinking, *this is our spiritual purpose on the planet*. When we choose non-forgiveness, judgments, and self-righteousness as our avenues and means of learning, we are denying that purpose. We are denying ourselves as spiritual beings who are granted full access to the kingdom of Heaven, and the Loving that is available through it.

Unfortunately, to empower the earthly church, most religions have taught their constituents to believe it is not in their power to ask for, institute, and receive forgiveness within their own consciousness, as a precursor to receiving the forgiveness that is *already always present for us in Spirit*. I love that Dr. Eben Alexander addressed this in his book, *Proof of Heaven*, which is about his experiences on "the other side" while he lay in an extended and

deep coma. He notes several times that his experience of that state, energy, beingness that I call Spirit (he called it OM) was:
1. We are always loved.
2. We are already forgiven.
3. We cannot do anything "wrong," in the sense that we cannot do anything that makes the first two precepts untrue.

He notes that all we must do is *claim that* as What Is for us on every level—and grant ourselves the same unconditional Loving, forgiveness, and grace that Spirit already grants us.

Forgiveness is the best teacher, or at least the most valuable tool for learning what we are here to learn: Loving. And yet, many of us place limitations on when this tool should be applied. We judge certain thoughts and behaviors as being too reprehensible to forgive. We practice forgiveness for minor offenses, but not for transgressions that truly result in pain and hurt.

Babinet once commented that, "Forgiveness is not the process of justifying the unjustifiable; it is simply a choice to move forward and allow the loving to be restored within our own consciousness, so that the acceptance, healing, and reprogramming can take place." In other words, practicing forgiveness is not a way of saying the thought or behavior that occurred was one of which we approved. Forgiveness is merely a means of allowing ourselves to reconnect with the loving inside of us; the Loving that is available to us through Spirit and the high self. From that place of Loving, our personal, relational, and situational healings can take place.

But, exactly how does forgiveness work, using the context of the Kahunas' system? In Huna, there is only one great sin which can be *consciously* committed. That sin is hurting another self. The high self is beyond the power of the lower self to hurt, so this applies to hurting either one's own low self or another person's. Hurting a self, any self, tends to create guilt, an emotion which causes the low self to block its connection with the high self. The low self, feeling guilt, and the shame and fear associated with it, does not expand out to contact the "Divine Being" that is its high self, as it feels unworthy of it. The high self is effectively the doorway to the Loving, wisdom, and guidance present for us through Spirit. When the middle and low selves do not align properly for this expansion and resultant connection, they are then effectively cut off from higher guidance, energy, and assistance.

Both Long and Hoffman specifically delineate that "hurting oneself" is to be included in the broad definition of hurting another self. Long specifies "hurting one's own body by excesses" or deprivation is a form of hurting one's self. Hoffman also points to the imposition of negative, guilt-producing beliefs on the low self by the middle self as a means of hurting one's self, because such beliefs cause the low self to judge itself by a rigid, dogmatic set of criteria.

Other forms of hurt the middle self often heaps on the low self is criticalness, name-calling, and demeaning tones and statements. Because of such treatment, the low self often feels guilt, shame, and fear just for *being*, and not for anything in particular that it has done. Many of us, according to Powell, in our inner conversations, practice some form of this self-abuse.

The Huna sin of "hurting others" is, perhaps, easier for us to understand. Most of us have already been taught to believe in some offshoot of it. The form of hurt inflicted on another self can be physical, emotional, mental, sexual, financial, and so on. It makes no difference. It is a "sin." The more intentional the hurt, the greater the sin. When we are fully aware that hurt will result from our actions, our guilt is greater. It is that sense of guilt that causes the low self to "flee from the face of God" (the high self), as a child flees from a parent when it knows it has done wrong and fears punishment may be given.

(An interesting side note here: according to Long, a person who is able to hurt others maliciously, feeling justified in doing that, with no sense of guilt, may not have his/her low self refuse to make contact with the high self. Nor will his/her high self cut him/her off. If that person prays for good things, the high self will respond. The retribution, so to speak, lies in this person—and his/her selves—finding that his/her upward evolution has slowed down.)

The Huna concept of sin is very much in keeping with Jesus' teaching, "Ye shall love thy neighbor as thyself" (Matthew 19:19). John-Roger rephrases this precept by saying, "Don't hurt yourself and don't hurt others." Honoring these teachings can lead us to a path that allows us to create more intimate, loving, functional relationships among all of our selves and the selves of others. Long calls this path simply, "Living a good and hurtless life."

For most of us, as basic as this may seem, living such a life is often more of a noble goal than a living reality. The concepts of it are fairly easy to understand, but not necessarily easy to follow. The states of our inner and outer relationships (between all of our selves and with the selves of others), attest to that. So, how can we possibly hope to enhance our connectedness with our high selves and enter the "kingdom of Heaven?"

We can practice *forgiveness*. In their book, *Life 101*, John-Roger and McWilliams define forgiving as meaning "for giving"--"for," in favor of; "giving," to give. They note that whether we are forgiving someone else or ourselves, we are always being "in favor of giving." We are *always* giving the state of forgiveness *to ourselves*.

Babinet notes that the word *forgiving* connotes a "moving forward" or a "forth giving." In the action of forgiving, we are choosing to give and to extend our loving. Forgiving opens a free-flowing channel of giving, and, out of that, receiving, which is very important in relationship to both the high self and the world. When we let go of negative feelings against ourselves and/or others, we open ourselves to the grace that is always present for us. Receiving is a natural outcome of our willingness to give up that negativity.

In forgiveness, there is always a flow of giving "up" into Spirit that which we have been holding onto and against ourselves or others. When we do that, Spirit gives back generously, inwardly and outwardly! John-Roger notes that through forgiveness "all things we want come to us in ways that are noble and honorable, for the best of us."

The forgiveness process is not a difficult one. We will outline several ways to approach it in PlayPages. However, before we move into alignment with that process and to ensure it takes place when we say the words, we must take some prerequisite steps.

Before we can forgive ourselves, or anyone else, we need to first acknowledge and accept what we have done and/or what has been done against us. We then need to acknowledge and accept the judgments we have placed against ourselves and against others. And, finally, we must acknowledge, accept, and experience the pain of having separated ourselves from our Loving, from our Hearts, and from Spirit.

Sometimes this process is done inwardly, within our own consciousness. Other times, as is noted in all "twelve-step" programs, we need to do it outwardly, in the form of "making amends" with other people involved in the situation. The goal of all this is to allow us to realize, fully and completely, the pain we have either caused or been experiencing. We need to garner the learning and wisdom that is present for us in that pain and then let it go.

There is an aspect of humility and honesty that seems to precede forgiveness. It is reflected in this process of acknowledgment and acceptance. John-Roger and McWilliams describe it this way, "All the things you think you should have done that you didn't do, and all the things you did that you think you shouldn't have done, accept them. You did (or didn't) do them. That's reality. That's what happened. There's no changing the past."

This is such a simplistic approach, but one that can put us in a better position to invite forgiveness. Louise Hay, in her book *You Can Heal Your Life* outlines a healing system based on relationships between the physical and psychological aspects of humans. She notes that the knees represent humility and surrender. Perhaps the archetypal posture from which we implore forgiveness, on our knees, affirms and symbolizes our need to surrender to the reality of the hurt we've caused or experienced.

And yet, often, even once we've accepted our responsibility in a situation (in which we either inflicted or received pain), our tendency is to rationalize and explain it away, making ourselves feel comfortable again, *consciously*. (We even do this as recipients of hurt, because acknowledging our pain, as "victims," means acknowledging our vulnerability—and that's uncomfortable.) At an unconscious level, however, within our low selves, we still know what we've done or what has been done against us. The hurt remains, and so does the guilt and accompanying shame, fear, and separation from the Loving. If we acknowledge, fully and consciously, our "sin" (or the "sin" of another against us), we can then let that go, releasing the separation and allowing the wholeness, Loving, and at-one-ment to be with us.

Again, let me illustrate how this works by using my own story. I was raised in an extremely emotionally and physically abusive family. The BEST part of my childhood was the five years (between ages five and ten) I spent in a state home/orphanage while my mom recovered from a psychological (schizophrenic) breakdown (her second). My dad disappeared when I was two, so I never knew him. When I lived with my mom and, after the orphanage, with her second husband, I was constantly told I was a "worthless piece of shit," and that I deserved to be abused and/or sent back to the orphanage (in other words, to be re-abandoned). Feeling angry or hating my parents would have been a perfectly normal human response.

However, if I felt or expressed anger or hurt or shock at the way my parents behaved, I was further abused or abused more harshly. My mother was very sensitive psychically and if I even showed an expression of emotion in my body posture or my face, she could read it and I would be punished. So, I learned to hide my feelings to a very extreme degree. That kept me safer.

But, that suppression had consequences. I was sick a lot, usually with respiratory illnesses or ear infections. (Louise Hayes notes these two illnesses as being about "suppressed crying," "anger," "not wanting to be here," "not wanting to hear the anger and turmoil expressed by parents.") I reached a point, at a very early age, where I could not feel my emotions any more. I did not even experience positive emotions. My emotions were simply flat, very close to non-existent. However, I was very able to experience my intellect. I was extremely good at learning information. But my understanding of information, people and life was not colored by emotional contexting.

Then, one day, after many years of receiving counseling, someone I was working with asked me, "What do you do with all your anger?" I was stunned. I did not consciously experience any anger, so I shrugged my shoulders. The counselor said, "You have every right to be angry. Those people were terrible to you."

The last phrase she said, giving me permission to be and feel angry and hurt, acted as a trigger. I immediately got a respiratory infection and a round of depression that lasted for six weeks. During that time, I found myself reviewing the counselor's words—and my childhood experiences. I began to feel an inkling of emotion about all that. Over the course of the next year or so, I got in touch with very deep and intense anger and rage. I took a workshop called "Model Mugging," which ripped that anger from my body memory where I had stuffed it, into a very conscious place in my mind and emotions, so I was able to look at it clearly and explore it further in counseling.

After several years of exploring the anger and hurt I felt at how I had been treated, I realized I did not want to live in that place, so I had to find my way through it. I began by working to understand my parents as people, with shortcomings, ignorance, and wounds of their own. That helped me. I developed a sense of compassion for them. Then I realized that to be compassionate toward myself,

I had to let go of all the harm they had done to me. I had to forgive them. I had to give up my hurt and anger.

Only by forgiving them and letting go of all of that negativity was I able to heal the hurt and the anger. Only then was I able to learn how to have a healthy relationship with myself and other human beings. I was able to be kind to my parents, even though I chose not to live near them and not to see them often, because they were still abusive in nearly every interaction. I had to put in physical boundaries, because they could not honor emotional boundaries in any way. But I was happy to be able to love them from a distance.

I was also able to love and forgive myself for having endured that part of my life. I was able to see and understand what I had learned from it. I even was shown the "pre-birth meeting" on the Other Side (in Spirit) at which I had agreed to endure that pain and hardship in order to get stronger in my Loving and Compassion for myself and other human beings. The meaning of the whole experience became clear to me.

I was also able to translate the awarenesses and emotional healing and growth I garnered through the exploring and healing of all that into being a far better parent than I would have been if I had stayed emotionally shutdown. I was a better parent than I would have been if I had simply "passed down" the hurt and anger to my children, as my parents had done, and as many people do. Instead, I was able to give my children profound Loving and wisdom. This was a much-desired outcome for me. Indeed, that was the true success of that situation—being a happy, whole, and healthy human being, and parenting/teaching my children to be that also.

It is important to realize that in Spirit, and through the high self, forgiveness is always present. It is an aspect of our Divine birthright. All we have to do is choose it. We need to stop separating ourselves from our hurt and anger, own it, heal it, let it go and, then, move back into alignment with the Loving, thus receiving it.

Forgiveness itself, however, may not be enough to facilitate this. Practicing forgiveness can lead us right to the gates of freedom from guilt, shame, and fear. It can even start the flow of Loving within us. But there is an additional step we must take, to ensure that the forgiveness anchors itself into the depths of our beings. To hold the state of grace that forgiveness bestows upon us, we must also *forget*. As John-Roger says, "You don't really get forgiveness *until you forget* what was blocking you from the Loving in the first place."

John-Roger and McWilliams define forgetting as "for-getting," being "in favor of getting, of receiving." In the world, if you have a clenched fist, it is difficult to receive. If you let go and open the fist, you have a hand. Then it is easy to receive.

To put this in Kahuna terms, if the low self is holding the memory of some transgression, either that it perpetrated or that was perpetrated against it, it will be contracted and withdrawn (remembering the pain). The physical body will want to constrict; the emotions will want to protect themselves. The low self will not be in the open, loving, trusting state it needs to be in to expand and connect with the high self. To truly receive the forgiveness, and thus move into expansion, the low self must give up the memory of the hurt. It must forget.

Forgive and forget. Come into a place of greater Light and Loving, laughter, and joy inside of you. Create and experience your life from that place. It's easy once you have given the judgments, guilt, fear, shame, and pain to Spirit! Through forgiveness and forgetting, all the bounty and the blessings become available to you! You receive the abundance of your spiritual heritage. That's a lot to be grateful for.

CHAPTER NINE
GRATITUDE

"There is no such thing as a problem without a gift for you in its hands." ~Bach

The American Heritage Dictionary defines grateful as "appreciative of benefits received." This definition is interesting to me because it presupposes that one is receiving "benefits." In my opinion, this offers us a key to experiencing the state of being grateful. To live in a state of gratefulness or gratitude, we also need to presuppose that we are receiving benefits.

To experience gratitude, we need to look at each experience we have, no matter how "challenging" it is, and glean the value that is hidden and inherent in it. We also need to interact with people in our lives, no matter how difficult they seem to be, as though they have a precious gift to offer us because when we look at them that way, they do! To experience gratitude, it is important that we always look beyond the obvious and visible in any situation or person, viewing every obstacle we encounter as a stepping stone to our greater freedom, Loving, and success. To do this, we simply need to perceive everyone and everything through our Hearts.

Remember, as Saint-Exupéry wrote, "It is only with the Heart that one can see rightly. What is essential is invisible to the eye."

Jesus, Buddha, Mohammed, and others have long instructed us to "count our blessings." But they didn't mention the reasons for doing this. One reason, of course (as noted above), is that counting our blessings causes us to view our lives differently, to develop a new and better perspective.

There is, however, another, more practical reason for being thankful. That reason is, "energy follows thought." What we see (or perceive) is what we get.

Our focus is a powerful magnet; we gravitate toward whatever we think about most. If a person has a lot of good stuff in his/her life and wants more but focuses primarily on what he/she doesn't have, "lack," he/she will get less and less of the good stuff and more of the "lack." (At least that is what he/she will notice.) Continuing with this thought, if a person focuses on something that he/she doesn't really want (something negative), he/she will get more of it, because that's where he/she is focused.

A wonderful example of this phenomenon, that many of us have probably experienced, is attempting to drive around a pothole in the road. If we notice a pothole in the road and try to miss it, we are completely focused on "missing the pothole," instead of "driving on the good part of the road." We will most likely hit the pothole, almost as though we are uncontrollably drawn to it. However, if we focus only on the part of the road we want to drive on, and then, simply drive, we'll do just fine, missing the pothole completely. We get what we focus on! Experiment with this the next time you find an asphalt crater in your path!

Our focus, and where we place it, can affect us in yet another way. At any given moment, there is ample evidence to prove that life is either a bed of thorns or a garden of roses. Generally, we base our decision about which it is, on how we *feel* about it. How we *feel* about life depends primarily on where we place our attention, that is, on *what we focus upon*.

Look around. Notice all the imperfections of your environment. How do you feel?

Look around you again. This time notice the good and the beautiful in that same environment. (If you find this challenging, and some people do, start by noticing that the chair, sofa or bed you are sitting or lying on is softer than a bed of nails! And go from there.) How do you feel now? Doesn't it feel better to be focused on the positive? Don't you feel capable of creating more good things from this state of appreciation?

When we want goodness in our lives, we need to begin by noticing all the goodness we have already created, promoted, allowed, invited, *and received*. When we do this, we realize that we are *obviously worthy* of receiving goodness, because we already have quite a bit of it. We also *feel capable* of creating more goodness, because we have evidenced our abilities to do that.

So, how does gratitude work in relationship to our middle and low selves? Let's explore that. The job of the middle self is to provide direction and focus for the low self. The middle self tells the low self what it should be creating. If the middle self is paying lots of attention to things it doesn't like or doesn't have yet, essentially, it is telling the low self to pay attention to that too.

This is especially true if the middle self is not giving the low self specific instructions on what it wants the low self to do with this awareness of negative or nonexistent things (instructions like, "Change that!"). If the middle self is just saying, "Look at this bad thing! Look at that 'lack!' Look at all of this stuff that isn't working!"—the low self has no idea what the middle self wants in relationship to everything it pointed out. The low self might think the middle self likes this "stuff" or thinks this "stuff" is important. The low self may even create more of it in an attempt to please its "Master," the middle self.

The low self's job, purely and simply, is to create what the middle self tells it to create. It uses previous experiences and the middle self's input to know how to do this. If the middle self does not direct the low self in a positive way and then give it specific directions on what and how to create, the low self will just recreate what it already knows—what it already has a recipe for! But, if the middle self notes, in great detail, exactly what it wants the low self to do, the low self will do that enthusiastically!

It works like this: the middle self says, "Wow! Remember that money we made last week? That was great! Let's make some more of it. Let's do this and this and this to get it. OK?!" The low self now knows exactly what the middle self wants created, and how it wants that done! The middle self has been really clear about "the project;" it even gave the low self a tangible example (the money we made last week). The middle self also outlined some possible ways the low self could get the job done. (The low self may have even more ideas that the two selves can discuss). There should be no problems in completing this enterprise, as long as both selves remain enthusiastic.

Which brings us to another benefit of being grateful. We've noted that gratitude allows the middle self to give the low self positive examples of what to create. But gratitude serves another valuable purpose for the lower selves. It makes them *feel good*!

In order for the middle self to appreciate the benefits it has received, it has to notice them. A middle self who doesn't believe that goodness and/or results are occurring in its life, gets evidence of them when it is counting its blessings. Thus, gratitude acts as a "prover" for a doubting middle self.

Gratitude also serves as an esteem builder for a discouraged, distrustful, unconfident low self, because the process itself demands that the middle self notice *positive accomplishments*. In acknowledging these accomplishments, the middle self, almost naturally, must acknowledge the low self. After all, the low self is the one who did *the work*, providing the energy and effort to complete the endeavors. The low self is also the one that channeled any miracles that resulted from collusion with the high self (in the form of extra energy and special guidance). Remember, high self participation is not possible without the low self!

So, when the middle self is handing out thanks, a large portion of them have to go to the low self. That appreciation enhances the low self's esteem, which increases its enthusiasm and desire to cooperate. These acts of appreciation, combined with the middle self's conscious acknowledgments of success, facilitate a better "*feeling*" relationship between the lower selves, empowering them to work together more smoothly and to effectively build the success we want in the future.

The attitude of gratitude also yields another, more profound piece to our success puzzle. Gratitude opens our Hearts. The middle self develops an appreciation for its own abundance, which it then shares with the low self. The low self, in receiving this appreciation, expands with the feeling of being acknowledged and loved. This expansion automatically leads to an increased connection with the Heart, and through that with the high self. That action brings forward a more evolved viewpoint of our life situations. This perspective increases our abilities to draw meaning, knowledge, and wisdom from our experiences, thus adding value to those experiences. In other words, in addition to allowing us to more clearly perceive the abundance that is already present in our lives, gratitude allows us to *add* to that abundance by amplifying our capacity for seeing with and through the Heart.

We perceive everything differently when we are grateful. Our inner success state is enhanced, because we view with satisfaction the abundance that is, and that has already been granted to us. By encouraging us to experience the abundance that has always been present for us, gratitude assists us in understanding, deeply, that we are loved and lovable human beings. We begin to perceive that the energy of Loving is at the very core of our existence. When we see clearly that everything we've ever wanted and needed has been given to us, we begin to grasp how completely we are loved and cared for—by Spirit, other people, ourselves, the world, and the Universe. After all, one doesn't give gifts and blessings to someone one hates or even feels neutral about. Goodness is given from Loving and valuing. So we can assume, from all the goodness we have already partaken of, that we are profoundly Loved and valued.

One final aspect of affirming the wealth and abundance that are ours, comes from counting the many "gifts of giving" that we receive. These are the contributions that we make to others, the opportunities we take to give of our plenty. The fact that we are capable and willing to give affirms even more that Loving is the core of our beingness. Through the gift of giving, we see, again, our innate value, and the vast reservoir of Loving, kindness, compassion, wisdom, and mercy that is available to and through us. We get to demonstrate that we have more than we need. By acknowledging and appreciating that which we give, as well as that which we receive, we bear witness to our own tremendous success. That's *a lot* to be grateful for!

CHAPTER TEN
SERVICE

"Do all the good you can,
   By all the means you can, in all the ways you can,
   In all the places you can,
   At all the times you can,
   To all the people you can,
   As long as you ever can." ~John Wesley

"Love isn't love 'til you give it away." ~greeting card

The first three steps in both Babinet's Movement of Loving and my own Flow of Loving are delineated as "connecting," "receiving" and "nurturing." These steps are the yin, or inner, aspects of the flow. They have to do with taking care of ourselves, connecting with the spiritual energy, receiving it into us, and becoming full of it. An aspect of the fourth step of the flow that begins to move from the inner to the outer, I term "expressing," and will discuss with the outer flow. (This is where I differ from Babinet's description of the Movement in my understanding and labeling of the "expressing" step.) Expressing is the point at which we become so filled with Loving and Spirit that it begins pouring through us and out into the world.

Service, as John-Roger and McWilliams define it in their books, is the art of taking such good care of ourselves that we cannot help but take care of others. When we are filled with Loving, and fulfilled in our own lives, we have more of everything than we need. The desire to share of our overflow is automatic. The beginning of this sharing of the overflow is "expressing." So, what is the best way to share it?

To answer this question, we need to understand that this "overflow" has two interesting qualities to it: first, it is abundant; and second, it can't be stored. It must be utilized as it is created and received. So, there is really only one way to share it—just *GIVE IT AWAY!* Give it to anyone and anything that happens to be present and in need of it, from wherever you are, in whatever ways you are capable of giving. Just give it away; be of *service*.

This giving of the overflow is actually quite a natural occurrence. Kahlil Gibran expresses this beautifully in his book, *The Prophet*:

> "You often say, 'I would give, but only
> to the deserving.
> The trees in your orchard say not so, not
> the flocks in your pasture.
> They give that they may live, for to withhold
> is to perish.
> Surely he who is worthy to receive his
> days and nights, is worthy of all else from you.
> And he who has deserved to drink from
> the ocean of life deserves to fill his cup
> from your little stream...

> "See first that you yourself deserve to be
> a giver, and an instrument of giving.
> For in truth it is life that gives onto
> life—while you, who deem yourself a giver,
> are but a witness."

As Gibran alludes, one of the great open secrets of life is that giving to others gives *us* more than we give away. By serving others we are serving ourselves. As Emerson states, "It is one of the beautiful compensations of this life that no one can sincerely try to help another without helping himself." John-Roger concurs when he notes that anyone who has ever given to others for the joy of giving knows that they are rewarded for that with *joy*. But what about those people who give for reasons other than the joy of giving? Gibran notes that their giving serves them also:

> "There are those who give little of the
> much they have—and they give it
> for recognition and their hidden desire
> makes their gifts unwholesome.
> And there are those who have little and
> give it all.
> These are the believers in life and the
> bounty of life, and their coffer is never
> empty.
> And there are those who give with joy, and
> that joy is their reward.
> And there are those who give with pain,
> and that pain is their baptism.
> And there are those who give and know

> not pain in giving, nor do they seek joy,
> nor give with mindfulness of virtue;
> They give as in yonder valley the myrtle
> breathes its fragrance into space.
> Through the hands of such as these God
> speaks, and from behind their eyes He
> smiles upon the earth."

Gibran also notes:

> "It is well to give when asked, but it is
> better to give unasked, through understanding;
> And to the open-handed the search for
> one who shall receive is a joy greater than giving."

For the "open-handed" Gibran speaks of, service is a selfish thing, in the truest sense of the word. It is done simply because it feels good, so good that one wants to do more and more. Service done in this mode is a blessing to both the giver and the receiver. Truly, this sort of giving exemplifies the saying, "The love I give you is second hand: I feel it first."

Those who have given to others and found it depleting, rather than fulfilling, most likely, have not taken the time to give fully to themselves first. Loving others from inner emptiness becomes a painful endeavor, seemingly a sacrifice. In his book, *Seat of the Soul*, Gary Zukav notes that people who love like this give love that is contaminated, filled with sorrow for themselves. It is important for us to connect to the Source of our Loving, the high self, our Soul and Spirit, and to practice loving and giving to ourselves before we give to others. This allows us to share loving that is pure in its essence, and easier for others to receive.

So, why don't we just do this "filling up" naturally and as a matter of course? According to the Huna concepts, people who do not and cannot "make the time" to connect with the high self or to give to themselves, are usually people who have a low self that is harboring guilt, shame, and fear. (See the chapter on "Forgiveness.") Such a low self is deliberately separating itself from the high self, the one that Spirit uses to fill us with pure, unlimited, unconditional, nourishing Loving. Consequently, the low self and, as a result of that, the middle self are cut off from that Loving and from spiritual guidance on how to more effectively love themselves. It is only when our low selves are connecting with our high selves (and, through that, Spirit) and experiencing being loved, and then Loving themselves that we are able to give to others, freely and naturally.

Once we have filled our own cups and are feeling loved, cherished, and cared for, we respond to seeing others in need of kindness, by wanting them to have it. We feel good about them receiving that. We want to be a part of giving them whatever they need. We instinctively want to give of the abundance inside of us. This is the nature and energy of Loving. This is the nature and energy of Spirit. This is Grace.

So, again, why do we often separate and deprive ourselves of this? Many types of judgments can serve to keep our low selves from reaching out to connect with our high selves. One of the most common is the judgment that we are unworthy because we have hurt another self. Doing service can actually assist us in clearing and releasing such guilt.

The Kahuna teachings repeatedly note that an important part of the forgiveness process is "making amends." It is stressed that, whenever possible, we should make these amends directly to the people we have injured. However, when this is not possible (because of death or distance or their unwillingness to participate), according to Max Freedom Long, "Good deeds (service) done unselfishly for others can be performed as vicarious atonement for hurt done to those who can no longer be reached to be asked for forgiveness, and to receive such things as can be offered as restitution or repayment."

In other words, our "random acts of kindness" and our deliberate good works can help to balance our own "karmic books." (Karma is defined by the American Heritage Dictionary as "the total effect of a person's actions or conduct...") Jesus seemed to concur. In Luke (4:46), he said, "Inasmuch as ye have done it (a kindly act) unto the least of these, thy brethren, ye have done it onto me." While no one else can pay our debts for us, we can obviously make our repayments to anyone who is handy and in need!

Seen in this light, it is easier to understand John-Roger's comment that "one of the greatest forms of service is letting others serve you." Just as we are gifting ourselves when we serve others, others, by being of service to us, are getting the opportunity to clear any debts they may have incurred through their behavior with others. They are also getting the good feelings and strengthened physiology and psychology that go with knowing one is capable of offering something good to another human being. We have only to look into the eyes of a person who has given something from his/her own Heart to another human being to recognize the blessings that are given when we allow someone to be of service to us.

In true service, the giver and the receiver are one. They are equals. By allowing others to serve us, we serve. By serving others, we are serving ourselves. It is a wonderful circle of giving and receiving. It becomes an endless flow. More than that, it becomes a stillness, a state of being, a place where Loving just is, and indeed, where we are the Loving.

I, myself, once had a wonderful experience of this phenomenon during a seminar designed to facilitate a deeper sense of Loving and service in the participants (Insight Seminars). It was a five-day training and by the middle of the last day, I still had not experienced anything particularly profound. There was one exercise left to do in the training. We were each to go out into the community and perform some act of service.

I wandered around the neighborhood (a suburb of New York City) for a while, unable to decide on a project. I happened upon a park. There were many "bums" and homeless people there. I felt inwardly directed to sit down and talk with one, a very dirty, older man. (This was quite a stretch for me, since I had been thoroughly indoctrinated not to talk to strange men. But, I was following my Heart!) I spent the next few hours caring for him. I fed him, bought him some extra food, washed his extra clothes at a near-by laundromat, bought him a jacket, walked and talked with him, and when I left, I gave him all the money I had in my wallet.

Somewhere in the midst of this exercise, I had a marvelous awakening. I suddenly realized that I was not only giving to this man, he was also giving to me, just by receiving my Loving and anything else I gave to him. The entire world became a beautiful river of Light, filled with giving and receiving everywhere. Every interaction I observed, or could think of, became simply an exchange of Loving. It was incredible!

Then, in another instant, all that ceased. The giving and receiving, the flow of Loving became a still, deep, endless pool. I was surrounded by it, immersed in it, and filled with it. Everything everywhere was Love. It and I were One, inseparable. I felt intoxicated, as though I would burst with the fullness—and then in a breath, I opened even more, becoming more One with the Loving. The experience went on and on and on, until it seemed like a natural state of beingness. It was a very enlightening, transformational exercise that will stay with me always.

I learned from that experience that whenever I feel limited, unsuccessful or non-abundant, I can challenge that feeling by *giving*. The action of giving affirms for me that Loving and abundance is always present for me, if I will just open to it. In fact, the easiest way for me to open to it is *to give*. I truly understand John-Roger and McWilliams' point of view that "the opening through which we give is the same opening through which we receive." When I expand my "opening"...my Heart...then I receive plenty, and more than I need.

Service is not a chore. It is a privilege. In truth, giving and receiving are both natural acts, and very human things to do. We need to receive mentally, emotionally, physically, sexually, financially, and so on in order to grow and be healthy. And when we are filled full from that receiving, our cup runneth over and, then, it hurts not to give.

Giving, like receiving, is fundamental to life. Harry Fosdick eloquently notes the importance of doing both in his book, *The Meaning of Service*:

"The Sea of Galilee and the Dead Sea are made of the same water. It flows down, clear and cool, from the heights of Herman and the roots of the cedars of Lebanon. The Sea of Galilee makes beauty of it,

for the Sea of Galilee has an outlet. It gets to give. It gathers its riches that it may pour them out again to fertilize the Jordan plain. But the Dead Sea with the same water makes horror. For the Dead Sea has no outlet. It gets to keep."

In the Flow of Loving, "receiving" is seen as the beginning of the cycle of Loving. Giving what is received out into the world ("action") is a natural completion to that cycle. It closes the circle of Loving, the Circle of Life.

That which we receive is the material we are given to build our lives. That which we give back becomes our means of truly recognizing who we are—Children of God. Our acts of giving are living affirmations that we are, like our Source and Creator, abundant and Loving, and capable of giving from that.

As David Spangler reminds us, "The only successful manifestation…(is the one that) has manifested God, or revealed Him more fully, as well as having manifested a form." As we become more aware of ourselves as spiritual beings, we will automatically manifest more and more of our success, both inner and outer. We will also discover that what we are really manifesting is God, as Love in action and form.

SECTION THREE PLAYPAGES

For this set of PlayPages, I've compiled a series of exercises that will assist you in having your own experience of the three processes we've just discussed. Each exercise notes which of the three you'll be exploring—forgiveness, gratitude or service. Each also comments on the specific purpose of that exercise. Track your results in your journal. And remember to have fun!

EXERCISE ONE
FORGIVENESS

To work with forgiveness, we need to understand the layers of judgments we heap upon ourselves. First, we judge the situation and/or the person involved in the situation (ourselves and/or someone else); next, we judge ourselves for having judged the situation and/or the person in the first place. Let me clarify what this might look like: My husband made the bed and didn't make it quite the way I liked. I thought (here's the first judgment!), "How stupid! (Now for the second judgment.) Men just can't do the simplest things right." Then I said, "Do I have to do everything?" (This is the third, "hidden," judgment that I'm superior!) And finally, noticing my husband's hurt look, I thought, (the fourth judgment), "What a witch I am! He was only trying to help."

All of these judgments need to be forgiven. The first three were against my husband and men in general. I judged that not making the bed my way was stupid. I judged my husband and men to be incompetent. I judged myself and my way of doing things as superior. The final judgment was against myself. I judged myself as "bad" for judging my husband and hurting his feelings. The result of all this would be *massive guilt and shame,* as well as separation from my high self and Spirit, unless I practiced layers of forgiveness.

To begin the forgiveness process, we need to discern what the layers of judgment are in relationship to a particular situation we want to clear and heal. Look back on an incident or interaction that has guilt or shame (or another negative emotion) attached to it. Note the uncomfortable feeling. Then, track back in your memory to locate the judgments that preceded these feelings. Write about those judgments in your journal.

1. Close your eyes. Do some gentle relaxation. Do the clearing visualization, having the low self invite the high self (and Spirit) to be present with you for the highest good as you do this exercise.
2. Then, simply say to yourself, "I forgive _____ (the name of the person, place or thing you judged, including yourself) for _____ (the "transgression"). I forgive myself for *judging*_____ *(the same* person, place or thing, including yourself) for _____ (whatever you judged)." Do that for each judgment.

3. Be still for a moment and let all of this "sink in." Then, open your eyes. Have your low self thank the high self for participating. As a middle self, thank your low self.
4. Do this as many times as necessary to completely release and clear the judgments. If the judgments are really powerful or have been held for a long time, it may take several repetitions to get the full effect.

That's the forgiveness process! It's very simple, but amazingly effective. If any feelings come up for you during this exercise, experience them. Those feelings signal that healing is taking place and that the sense of separation is leaving.

EXERCISE TWO
FORGIVENESS

(The next technique is suggested by Dr. Bertrand Babinet.)

1. Close your eyes. Do some gentle relaxation. Do the clearing visualization with the low self. Have it invite the high self to connect with you and to stay present as you do this exercise.
2. Repeat out loud or write these affirmations:
    - I forgive myself for all judgments I hold against myself or anyone else, in relation to anything I have seen or not seen, that I am seeing or not seeing, or that I am afraid or want to see or not see.
    - I forgive myself for all judgments I hold against myself or anyone else, in relation to anything I have heard or

not heard, that I am hearing or not hearing, or that I am afraid or want to hear or not hear.
- I forgive myself for all judgments I hold against myself or anyone else, in relation to anything I have felt or not felt, that I am feeling or not feeling, or that I am afraid or want to feel or not feel.
- I forgive myself for all judgments I hold against myself or anyone else, in relation to anything I have said or not said, that I am saying or not saying, or that I am afraid or want to say or not say.
- I forgive myself for all judgments I hold against myself or anyone else, in relation to anything I have done or not done, that I am doing or not doing, or that I am afraid or want to do or not do.
- I forgive myself for all judgments I hold against myself or anyone else, in relation to anything I have smelled or not smelled, am smelling or not smelling, or that I am afraid of or want to smell or not smell.
- I forgive myself for all judgments I hold against myself or anyone else, in relation to anything I've touched or not touched, that I am touching or not touching, and everything I am afraid or want to touch or not touch.

A shortcut to all of these might be: I forgive myself for all judgments I hold against myself or anyone else, in relation to anything I have experienced or not experienced, that I am experiencing or not experiencing, or that I am afraid or want to experience or not experience.

(These affirmations often bring specific situations into our consciousness, because as the low self releases the judgment, it also releases the memory from its ectoplasmic field. Exercise One can be used to forgive the specific judgments of the specific situation. The more exact we are about the judgments we are clearing, the more effective the forgiveness process becomes.)

3. Let whatever feelings come up for you as a result of doing this process, surface, and be released.
4. In closing, have the low self thank the high self. Then, as a middle self, thank the low self for participating.

EXERCISE THREE
FORGIVENESS

(This is more of an addendum to the previous exercises than an exercise in itself. It is suggested by John-Roger and McWilliams in You Can't Afford the Luxury of a Negative Thought.*)*

1. Ask the high self to be present with you for the Highest Good. (This can be done informally, as a simple invocation.)
2. Declare regular periods of General Amnesty during the day. Forgive yourself and anyone else for anything that happened or failed to happen, since the last General Amnesty or forgiveness exercise. Just say, "I forgive _____ (whoever) for _____ (whatever). I forgive myself for judging _____ (whoever) for _____ (whatever)." Schedule these every few hours. Nothing from your past is worth polluting your present any longer.
3. Always thank your high self and your low self for participating.

EXERCISE FOUR
GRATITUDE
MATERIALS: Pen and your journal

1. Make a list of everything and everyone in your life that you are grateful for. These people, things, experiences and/or circumstances can be currently present in your life, or they may have been in your past. If you have ever had them and enjoyed them, list them. The items on your list can be tangible real-life objects and experiences or they can be intangible inner qualities and circumstances (i.e. a sense of peace).

2. List these items by writing sentences, each starting with a phrase like, "I am grateful for..." or "I am thankful for..." Fill in the blank at the end of the sentence with the name of the item, person or experience for which you are thankful. It is important to write the sentence out, in full, for each item. Remember, the low self learns from repetition. As much as this exercise is a reminder of the good things in your life, it is also an affirmation of all that goodness.

3. Ask all the parts of you, all of your selves, to participate with you on this exercise. Be thorough. Take your time, and explore your life in minute detail. Ask a zillion questions. One question I would suggest including is, "What experiences or people have I had in my life that I hated or found less than pleasurable (or that simply bugged me), from which or from whom I gained some valuable awareness, insight or

information about myself or life in general?" Some great gifts and blessings can be discovered by asking that question.
4. Write in your journal about anything you observe or learn from this exercise. This is a great way to clarify and thoroughly *receive* the incredible abundance that is, and always has been, present in your life.

EXERCISE FIVE
GRATITUDE
MATERIALS: Pen and your journal

A second important element of experiencing the state of gratitude is to be thankful for all that we have been permitted to give or contribute in our lives. Ask yourself, What have you *accomplished* or *achieved* that you can be grateful for? Make a list. Anything you have contributed to or achieved in any way, in relationship to yourself, another person or the world as a whole, counts. These items can be as simple as learning to walk (giving yourself the gift of mobility), as impressive as graduating from medical school (giving yourself a degree and a great career, as well as giving the world another doctor/healer) or as personally profound as giving birth to a child or saving another person's life. Write everything down. Begin each sentence with, again, "I am grateful for..." or "I am thankful for..."

Most of us have accomplished and contributed more than we realize. This exercise can allow us to consider the amount of value that we have to offer, the number of blessings that have come through us to the world, and to be grateful for that. Being grateful for what we have accomplished or given—and the privilege of doing that—is as important as being thankful for what we have received.

Have all your selves work with you on this. Search all the nooks and crannies of your life unearthing the treasure throve of achievements you may not ever have acknowledged before. Realize that all of this is a statement of your value, of what you have to offer and give. Every bit of it is something to be grateful for. Savor it!

EXERCISE SIX
GRATITUDE
MATERIALS: Pen and your journal

1. At the end of each day, do one of the exercises or suggestions from Chapter Two that assists you in centering in your Heart and accessing your Loving.
2. Look back over your day. Review a few situations, some pleasant and some more difficult. Discern the blessings present in those situations and with the people involved. Write them in your journal, beginning each entry with, "I am grateful for..."
3. Observe how that changes your feelings toward, and your perceptions of, these experiences and people.
4. A similar exercise can be done by viewing only the people in your life. Look at them all, the "easy" ones and the more "difficult." What gifts are available to you through each of them?
5. Note your perceptions in your journal. Doing these exercises every day will assist you in developing a new perspective.

EXERCISE SEVEN
SERVICE
PURPOSE: Connecting with Spirit

1. Meditate. There are many forms of meditation. Experiment and explore until you find one that works for you.
2. Contemplate. Contemplation is thinking about something of an uplifting nature. Ponder a concept or quality that is important to you. Contemplate a quote or idea that you find expansive. Contemplate an object, such as a flower or a rock.
3. Invocate. Talk to your higher power, whatever that force is for you, however you experience it. Pray.

EXERCISE EIGHT
SERVICE
PURPOSE: Loving and caring for yourself

1. Make a list of things you enjoy. Give yourself the pleasure of doing these things often.
2. Appreciate these things.

EXERCISE NINE
SERVICE
PURPOSE: Loving and caring for yourself

Be nice to yourself, and everyone and everything else. Forget the way things "should," "must" or "ought" to be.

EXERCISE TEN
SERVICE
PURPOSE: Loving and caring for yourself

1. Practice patience, acceptance, loving, kindness, forgiveness, caring, ease, grace, and surrender.
2. Pick one of these qualities each week. Write that word on index cards or Post-its. Put these in places where you will see them often, reminding you to experience and express that quality.

EXERCISE ELEVEN
SERVICE
PURPOSE: Loving and caring for yourself

1. Every night before bed, make a list of ten good things that happened that day.
2. Remember the joy and pleasure of them.

EXERCISE TWELVE
SERVICE
PURPOSE: Loving and caring for yourself

1. Breathe in and out. Do it again. Relax your body. Let go of disturbing thoughts and feelings. Feel good. Think happy thoughts.
2. Repeat this often.

EXERCISE THIRTEEN
SERVICE
PURPOSE: Letting others serve you

1. Every time someone does something nice for you, say "thank you." Receive it, with no explanations or excuses

or apologies. If a gift is being given to you, it's yours. You deserve it. Know that. Say it out loud if you need to, "I deserve this. I am worthy of receiving this goodness."

2. Make a list of things you need assistance from other people to complete. Align with your Heart and allow your intuition to tell you who to ask to assist you, then ask them. Notice their response. When they assist you, say "thank you" and affirm your worthiness.

EXERCISE FOURTEEN
SERVICE
PURPOSE: Serving others

1. Connect with your Heart and your Loving. Think about the people in your life. What do they need from you? Is there anything you could do to make their life easier, happier, healthier, and more fun? Make a list of potential service opportunities.

2. Ask the people involved if you can assist them in the particular ways you thought they might like. Be strong and clear in your willingness and desire to serve them, and honor their response. If they choose not to take you up on it, move on to the next possibility on your list. It is not loving to force kindness on someone who doesn't want or can't accept it or to help someone who wants to "do it myself." If you came up with service that can be done anonymously, do that. The gift of anonymous service lies purely in the doing, not in any acknowledgment you might get. As John-Roger says, "Do good work. Do it in the name of Loving. Let your own name become silent."

3. Watch for opportunities to do good works throughout your days. Spontaneous service, such as helping the proverbial little old lady across the street and carrying her sack of groceries, can make each day more special.

These are, of course, just a few of the exercises we can do to gain the experiences of forgiveness, gratitude, and service. Feel free to make up your own or to discover others. The most important part of these exercises is savoring the feelings, and the state of being they bring forward inside of you. Forgiveness, gratitude, and service can assist us in achieving deeper communion and higher levels of cooperation with each other. These processes can also allow us to experience greater Loving for ourselves, and for others. This benefit may truly be the most accurate indicator of our success.

SECTION FOUR

THE OUTER FLOW OF LOVING: MANIFESTATION

Prelude to Section Four

"To have abundance in Soul does not mean having lots of things, it means having access to and communion with the Essence of all things. Once you are in touch with that, you have the potential for and the experience of all things inside yourself. You don't feel any lack. You have fullness and gratitude. You walk free knowing that whatever you need will come to you." ~John-Roger and Paul Kaye

"What we achieve inwardly will change outer reality." ~Plutarch

"It is a matter of loving yourself enough to clarify and clear the channels so that your success can manifest in reality here, in this lifetime, for you to have, enjoy, and share." ~John-Roger

"If I chase it, I separate into the Chaser and the Chased. If I am it, I am it and nothing else." ~John C. Lilly

So, at this point, if we have done the work outlined in these first three sections, we have fulfilled the intention of the book, which was to allow, encourage, and enable each one of us to access our experience of Loving, which is the Heart of our success. Beyond this point, what we are talking about is manifestation, or the creation of form, and substance, actions, and words that carry our unique and individual expression of Loving out into the world to benefit ourselves and others.

It is critical to understand that if one does the inner work, thus consciously tapping into the Loving energy that is the Source energy, and if we invite and allow that energy to *fill us*, and if our low and high self become an effective mechanism for that process, we have mastered the Heart and essence of success. For that *is* true success—being the Loving, and knowing and experiencing that every day.

When one follows the inner flow of Loving, one naturally experiences fullness, joy, abundance, being loved, loving, richness, and access to all the limitless possibilities of the Universe. One walks around *full* and experiencing *enoughness*—actually, more than enoughness, *overflow*! One can then practice the outer flow of Loving into *manifestation*, if one is directed and inspired to do that, though it may become almost superfluous and unnecessary. Once one is *full* of the Loving that is *all* and *everything*; one experiences no lack. One knows that one is loved and cared for, that one is the essence of all things, has access to all things, and there is nothing to prove and no sense of emptiness to fill up, no need to satisfy.

And, that said, manifestation can be *fun*. It can be satisfying. It can allow us to provide ourselves with experiences and "stuff" that can make the physical world easier and more pleasing for ourselves. It can allow us to assist and support others.

Manifestation is good. It can be God. It can also be the Loving.

CHAPTER ELEVEN
EXPRESSING AND ENVISIONING

> "Prosperity—which means health, wealth, and happiness to me— must come from inside and then manifest outside in the world. You can live your own prosperity, but first you must discover it inside of you." ~ John-Roger

Once we have done the inner work and completed the inner flow of Loving, it is time for us to bring the fullness of Spirit's Loving and our Loving for ourselves into the world in a manifested form that benefits us and, hopefully, others also. This manifested form then becomes our outer or worldly success. This aspect of creating success is the outer flow of Loving, for, indeed, if it is done correctly and in alignment with our inner state that is now *full* of the Loving Energy of the Universe, our outer manifestation will match.

This is where my version of the Flow of Loving deviates the most from Babinet's original model. From my experience, the outer flow of Loving manifests first as expressing. Then it comes forward as envisioning, planning/practical reasoning, and *action!* Let's explore these four steps.

Expressing, as I mentioned in Chapter Ten, is the beginning of the outer flow of Loving through the human consciousness and out into the world. It happens naturally. As the Loving flows from Spirit, through the high self into the low self, the low self becomes *full*. The energy of Loving begins to overflow out to others and the world as giving. There is an aspect of this that is simply loving expression—joy, laughter, playfulness, compassion, and generosity. This, from my experience, is the first step in the outer flow of Loving.

The next step of the outer flow is about the low self being so connected to the high self—in its innate joy, playfulness, creativity, and compassion—that it can easily perceive the high self's vision, thus discerning Spirit's greater plan for us, our higher destinies, more or less, the Master Blueprints for our roles and places in the world. I call this step "envisioning." When that vision for our lives is brought forward from a low self that is filled with the awareness and experience that it is *loved* and *rich* simply because it exists in a universe that is Loving and rich, the vision that comes forward and the dreams that the low self has about what to do here on Earth have a very different quality than those from a low self that feels unloved, selfishly or unhealthily loved, neglected, abused, forgotten, or poor. What the low self wants is different when it is *gloriously full* from the inside-out.

By cultivating the natural and intended relationship between our high selves and our lower selves, we begin to transform the quality of our dreams, our visions, our concepts of what we are capable of in the world. The highest vision for us and our lives is one that is held in Spirit for us. That vision can be brought to us through the high self and it can be communicated—planted, as a conceptual seed, in the low self, which is our subconscious mind and essentially our Inner Child. This is truly the most creative aspect of our human selves. Looked at this way, the quote about,

"And the little child will lead us," has a different meaning and makes a lot more sense.

And, in order to access this information, this dream, this seed, this vision—we, as conscious middle selves need to have a *healthy* relationship with our low selves, our inner children. We need to hear and listen to them, give the ideas that come out of them credence, and actually be open to the idea that this aspect of ourselves has something valuable to share with us. Yes, the inner child is also an aspect of us that can be silly and playful, and sometimes it needs guidance on how to "play" in the world in healthy ways. Just as loving parents do for actual children, as responsible middle selves, it is our job to both allow the natural joy and playfulness of the low self to express here, and also to guide the low self when its behavior, focus or expression is immature or harmful in some way. It is also our job as conscious selves to encourage the creativity of the low selves to express in its most positive form. Like actual children, even the healthiest low selves can inadvertently express and behave inappropriately. So, we want to listen and heed the inherent wisdom, creativity, and innovativeness of the inner child, but as middle selves, as adults, with perhaps greater knowledge of the world, we also want to guide them—and we want to shape how the vision they receive moves out into the world.

But, that does not mean stifling the low self. When the low self is filled to tip-top with the sense and state of being *loved, rich, and happy*, it will naturally move into positive expression. This positive expression will be much like what we see in healthy, happy children—enthusiasm, joy, playfulness, fun, confidence, trust, openness, an innate sense that all is right with everything, and the feeling that they can accomplish/do anything. That form of expression is dynamic, uplifting, and motivational for the individual. It also manifests as charisma and inspiration to others in the world. These latter qualities are invaluable for getting other people's assistance in manifesting your vision of success!

Now we are ready to discuss the role of practical reasoning/planning in the Outer Flow of Loving, and then action, as a key element in the manifestation of our success.

CHAPTER TWELVE
PRACTICAL REASONING/PLANNING

> "A wise man bridges the gap by laying out the path by which he can get from where he is to where he wants to be." ~John Pierpont Morgan

The next two elements of the Outer Flow of the Loving are by their nature action steps. Therefore, these chapters will be somewhat short. I will not be doing PlayPages for them as there are many books that address this outer aspect of creation.

Once the low self is overflowing with loving, enthusiasm, creativity, and a sense of well-being, and it is filled with the vision of what is possible in life and the world, the natural next step is that it will communicate that to the middle self. It is a simple truth that the middle self has to be listening and open to hear what the low self has to say. There are a number of simple tools that can be used in this communication process—a journal, vision-boards, free-form writing or sketching of the low self's ideas.

The important piece here is to realize that this piece is the middle self's job in the success process. Once the low self has communicated and clarified its vision, usually in some fun way, of what can be created, of what is possible, the middle self needs to take that vision, fine-tune it, and figure out how to get it done in the real world. The low self, again, because it is very much like a child, should not be in charge of this piece, except for possibly offering creative ideas when the middle self gets stumped on how to get things done.

So, vision in hand, the middle self needs to apply practical reasoning and develop a plan on how to make the low self's vision a living reality here. There are many fine books and classes available to help one learn these practical steps.

CHAPTER THIRTEEN
ACTION

"Vision without action is merely a dream. Action without vision merely passes time. A vision with action can change the world!" ~Joel A Barker

In the final step—"action"—we actually do whatever it takes to bring forward our vision into a living creation. Period. We follow our plan, as delineated by the middle self, dealing with all obstacles and making any necessary adjustments to completion!

Then we celebrate! We acknowledge ourselves for doing a great job!

YAY US!

CLOSING

"The Spirit will give you that which is your intention,
And the amazing thing is
You can't put your intention out into the world.
It's for you, it's your own universe to live in.
If you are not creating a healthy (wealthy and happy) universe,
That will eventually show up out in your world.
You will have catastrophe and disaster,
as well as poverty, ill-health, mental disturbances and emotional pain." ~John-Roger

Present the world with Love. Build Loving to be a Source and foundation so securely inside yourself that nothing can shake it. Love all of your selves. View every aspect of yourself and every person and situation in your life through the eyes of Love. Give everything to Love. That's the key to health, wealth, happiness, and success!

EPILOGUE

Someone suggested that I take a moment, in closing, to list my personal successes as a result of using the system outlined in this book. So, my list of things most people would note as successes:

- I am healthy, attractive and happy.
- I raised four beautiful daughters, mostly alone, to be healthy, wealthy, happy human beings, who consider me to be not only their mom, but also their friend.
- I have four (almost five) amazing grandchildren.
- I have had a variety of satisfying, lucrative, fun careers. I have done well in all of them.
- I have an MA in Psychology and an MT in Theology.
- I have received numerous awards for excellence and service.
- I have had numerous licenses in various fields.
- I owned my own lovely four-bedroom home for twenty-six years.
- I drive a nice car.
- I am in a healthy, happy long-term relationship.
- I have taken a lot of wonderful national and international vacations.

- I have a lot of great, true friends.
- I am respected by a large community of peers.

To be clear, all those things and experiences are simply *manifestations* I get to experience in the world. They are all wonderful and satisfying! I am very grateful for all of them.

But, to me, the most important result of utilizing this system is that despite challenging, somewhat difficult, early life experiences—and a *lot* of negative programming from family and caretakers during that time, I am at my core a truly kind, loving, confident person. I have great Peace inside of me. I am full of goodness, hope and joy, and I express that freely with everyone who touches my life in any way. I am open, vulnerable, sensitive and empathic. I am also strong and free in every way. I take good care of myself and others. I care deeply about people, as well as myself—and I am comfortable with that. I have a GREAT sense of humor, which I access and share even when the going gets rough (as it always does at some points in life).

I am understanding and kind to/with myself and others, even in times of duress and distress. When I disagree with someone, I can accept the differences between us with compassion and understanding. I can assist people in experiencing compassion and understanding with themselves and others.

I actively experience that Spirit, and my own Soul, are always present in my life, guiding, protecting and humoring me. I learn from every situation and circumstance in my life. No matter what, I move forward in a positive manner, and I use every experience as a way of deepening my loving for myself and others. I allow my life experiences to be growth-full and uplifting. I experience goodness in my life in a very powerful way. Even when times are difficult, I ask for and envision only goodness for myself and others, and I do the planning and work to make that happen.

All of that comprises the most important aspects of my success. Indeed, all of that is the Heart of my Success.

About the Author

Virginia has worked as a psychological-spiritual counselor and class facilitator for over forty years. She has had the Gift of Seeing into Spirit/the Other Side since birth, and was able to use that effectively in the counseling arena. She has also played a lot in the business arena and enjoys expressing her creative nature through painting, writing, music and dance. She lives and works "outside the box" and is also very practical in her approach to life. She enjoys a rich, deeply satisfying life full of people she loves, including her Life Partner, four grown daughters, quite a few grandchildren and quite a few Heart Friends. She loves to travel. She holds degrees and accreditation in MA Psychology, Regis University; MT Theology, PTS Seminary; Master Level NLP Practitioner; DISC personality profile administrator; CMT; MSIA Minister. She began her spiritual quest when she was twenty-one, and, since then, has made a practice of being of Loving Service to Spirit and the World.